Remembering and Resisting

Remembering and Resisting

—— The New Political Theology ——

Johann Baptist Metz

EDITED BY
John K. Downey

CASCADE *Books* · Eugene, Oregon

REMEMBERING AND RESISTING
The New Political Theology

Cascade Books
An Imprint of Wipf and Stock Publishers
199 W. 8th Ave., Suite 3
Eugene, OR 97401

www.wipfandstock.com

PAPERBACK ISBN: 978-1-6667-1030-4
HARDCOVER ISBN: 978-1-6667-1031-1
EBOOK ISBN: 978-1-6667-1032-8

Cataloguing-in-Publication data:

Names: Metz, Johann Baptist, 1928–2019, author. | Downey, John K., 1948–, editor.

Title: Remembering and resisting : the new political theology / by Johann Baptist Metz ; edited by John K. Downey.

Description: Eugene, OR : Cascade Books, 2022 | Includes bibliographical references.

Identifiers: ISBN 978-1-6667-1030-4 (paperback) | ISBN 978-1-6667-1031-1 (hardcover) | ISBN 978-1-6667-1032-8 (ebook)

Subjects: LCSH: Political theology. | Catholic Church—Doctrines.

Classification: BT83.59 .M47 2022 (print) | BT83.59 .M47 (ebook)

08/16/22

Ashley, J. Matthew. "Remembering Johann Baptist Metz." *America: The Jesuit Review*, December 3, 2019. Reprinted with permission of America Press, Inc.

"Between Remembering and Forgetting: The Shoa in the Era of Cultural Amnesia." In *Good and Evil After Auschwitz: Ethical Implications for Today,* edited by Jack Bemporad, John T. Pawlikowski, Joseph Sievers, 21–28. Translated by Leo Penta. Hoboken: KTAV, 2000. Reprinted with permission of KTAV Publishers and Distributors.

"Elephant mit Hoffnung." Interview by Michael Jackqueman. *Katholische Nachrichten-Agentur* (November 23, 2000) 1–2. Translated by John K. Downey and published here as "The Elephant with Hope" with permission of Katholische Nachrichten-Agentur.

"Facing the World: A Theological and Biographical Inquiry." Translated by John K. Downey. *Theological Studies* 75.1 (2014) 23–33. Reprinted with permission.

"God and the Evil of This World. Forgotten, Unforgettable Theodicy." In *The Return of the Plague*, edited by José Oscar Beozzo and Virgil Elizando, 3–17. *Concilium* 5. Maryknoll: Orbis, 1997. Reprinted with permission of Concilium Secretariat, Paris, France.

"In Memory of the Other's Suffering: Theological Reflections on the Future of Faith and Culture." In *The Critical Spirit: Theology at the Crossroads of Faith and Culture*, edited by Andrew Pierce and Geraldine Smyth, OP, 179–88. Translated by Peter Kenny. Dublin: Columba, 2003. Reprinted with permission of Andrew Pierce and Geraldine Smyth.

"Memoria Passionis als Grundkategorie Politischer Theologie." In *Memoria Passionis: Ein provozierendes Gedächtnis in pluralistischer Gesellschaft*, 252–57. Freiburg: Herder, 2006. Translated by John K. Downey and published here as "Memoria Passionis: A Fundamental Category of Political Theology" with permission of Verlag Herder.

"Über Gott und das Glück." Interview by Jürgen Manemann. *Theologie der Gegenwart* 49.2 (2006) 124–25. Translated by John K. Downey and published here as "On God and Happiness" with permission of *Theologie der Gegenwart*.

"Dieser Papst ist für Überraschungen gut." In *Gespräche, Interviews, Antworten*, 219–23. Interview by Alexander Kissler. Freiburg: Herder, 2017. Translated by John K. Downey and publishered here as "This Pope is Good for a Few Surprises" with permission of Verlag Herder.

"Under the Spell of Cultural Amnesia?" In *Missing God?: Cultural Amnesia and Political Theology*, edited by John K. Downey, Jürgen Manemann, and Steven T. Ostovich, 5–10. Translated by John K. Downey and Steven Ostovich. Münster: Lit Verlag, 2006. Reprinted with permission of Lit Verlag.

"Aufwachen, Augen öffnen, Leid erkennen." Interview by Peter Rappert. In *Gespräche, Interviews, Antworten*, 210–14. Freiburg: Herder, 2017. Translated by John K. Downey and publishered here as "Wake Up, Open Your Eyes, See the Suffering" with permission of Verlag Herder.

For Meara Nelson Downey,
who believed in giving people chances

Contents

CONTENTS

Preface

Breathing Air from the Future

THESE ESSAYS AND INTERVIEWS are an invitation to consider our future. Where are we headed and what do we stand for? The political theology of Johann Baptist Metz emerged as an attempt to thrive amid shifting borders and threatening situations. It does not prescribe particular policies or a political agenda, but it does ask where we are and where we might stand in order to shape a meaningful future together. Theology is a culture of questions. And the most basic question for human life and theology is the question of theodicy, the question to God about human suffering.

Human history is a history of suffering. The person of faith will always miss God in that suffering, will ask where God has gone, or why God is not there. For Metz, these troubles cannot be dissolved through some sort of "justification of God." Suffering remains something that should not be (Job). Metz calls on us to see and confront the abysmal suffering in the world. How can we even speak of God in such a world? And so theodicy becomes not a question *about* God but rather a question *to* God. At the same time, we are drawn to connect with others, even with strangers: their suffering has a certain authority, and it places a claim on us. Jesus insisted—in line with his Jewish tradition—that love of God and love of neighbor reflect each other.[1]

---

1. "For me, there is no God to whom I could pray with my back turned to Auschwitz. When that became clear to me, I tried no longer to engage in

PREFACE

The universalism of our compassion is based on the universalism of human suffering. Jesus' parable of the Good Samaritan insists that the neighbor for whom we are responsible is whoever is there: not just our kin, not just our church, not just our class or political party, not just those like us. Rather, "neighbor" expands outward to include any who are suffering. This tentative practical solidarity is the first step into the future.

We are one before the threat of unjust suffering and evil: we all face this prospect. The point of solidarity is not just to remember suffering but to effect the changes needed to end it and to claim our hope by joining with others. In communion, we attack the erasure of human beings in the imagined borders projected by racism, xenophobia, nationalism, sexism, and other techniques of domination and fear. Reason in theology remembers, it is anamnestic. It also refuses to make the other invisible through domination. Here lies our common ground: in waking up and opening our eyes.

By asking how to relate to each other and to God, we find bedrock. Our spade is turned: we come to see that we stand for compassion, for an active connection with the "other." The memory of suffering becomes dangerous because it leads us to compassion, and compassion takes us out of isolation and out of our comfort zone; it challenges us to respond to suffering. Compassion changes us by making us aware that we live and breathe within a matrix of relationships.

A Christian political theology will ask questions about human dignity and suffering in any and all situations and theories. Who is hurt? Who will suffer? Who will be invisible? Bringing the experience of suffering forward as a touchstone offers the chance to strive for a different future and to affirm our hope. The present is only provisional.

---

theology with my back turned to the invisible, or forcefully made invisible, sufferings in the world; neither with my back to the Holocaust nor with my back turned to the speechless sufferings of the poor and oppressed in the world. This probably was the starting point toward the construction of a so-called political theology" (Metz, "Facing the Jews," 41).

Metz has famously asserted that the shortest definition of religion is interruption. That interruption, confronting the suffering in God's world, is unsettling because it questions God's promises as well as our own humanity. Of course religion brings comfort, but we must be careful that the comfort we find does not hide reality but brings us to engage it. We need a comfort that asks after God and misses God, that does not forbid grief and melancholy, that is not obsessed with denying the real suffering in the world, that is not a cover for an apathetic rationality, that does not avoid taboo questions about our solidarity with the dead, that does not hide the emptiness of a human future with optimism about progress.

There is the very human distaste for the different, for "them" over against our designated "us." But, as the parable of the Good Samaritan suggests (and contemporary neuroscience and evolutionary theory affirm[2]), we can adjust who is a "we" and who is a "they" and thereby expand who matters. Political theology is nothing other than an attempt to hear the voice of the biblical God of the tradition in these, our own times.

For Metz, the important criterion for theology is whether it denies or respects human solidarity. Human connection makes ethical claims, and Christians are called to show their connectedness in their actions: to be mature and responsible, to be doers, actors, agents, and not mere passive objects bobbing atop the waters of history. The memory and solidarity for which Metz calls includes not only critical grief and active compassion, but also a hope that connects all people. It turns out that asking about suffering is transformative.

Paradoxically, at a time when we have never known more about our globe or shared more information, we live in a riven, disconnected world. Diversity ends in mere juxtaposition of "others" or even in the domination over those who differ. In science, in economics, and in our communications industry, the human person tends to disappear from consideration or evaporate into an abstraction. The new political theology tries to break the spell of

2. For the neurobiology, see Sapolsky, *Behave*. An interesting review of the evolutionary biology is Christakis, *Blueprint*.

this cultural amnesia. This is the contribution of political theology: we can breathe new air that comes from the future.

The essays and interviews collected here crisscross the terrain of the new political theology from various directions.[3] Some of these chapters draw a general picture of political theology while others focus on a key idea. In the first chapter, Metz provides an overview of his theological development. Along the way, I include several interviews with him because they have a way of getting to the point without too much theological baggage. The final essay is an obituary written by Matthew Ashley of Notre Dame University, an important translator and friend of Metz. His rich reflection provides a feel for the context and trajectory Metz's theological questioning. Johann Baptist Metz wants to engage us in dangerous memories and move us to respond to the lure of a new future. Enjoy the conversation.

John K. Downey

3. For more readings and background, see www.johannbaptistmetz.com.

Acknowledgments

THANKS TO ADAM MCINTURF of Wipf and Stock for proposing this book project, and to my editor at Wipf and Stock, Charlie Collier, for his careful guidance. Jackie Fulton, Religious Studies Faculty Assistant at Gonzaga University, went out of her way to help with the preparation of the texts for publication. My colleagues Alexis Nelson and Inga Jablonsky, formerly of Spokane Falls Community College, provided consistently insightful comments. I am grateful for the humor and friendship of Johann Baptist Metz. May he continue to disturb us.

Part I

A Theology of the World

CHAPTER I

Facing the World

A Theological and Biographical Inquiry

MY THEOLOGICAL BIOGRAPHY IS inscribed with one name above all: Karl Rahner, my teacher and friend. Through him I entered the weave of the Catholic theological tradition. When Rahner died in 1984, he was considered by many to be the most significant and influential Catholic theologian of his time and a tremendous inspiration and challenge for his church. If Catholic theology today sees more and sees differently than he did, this is so largely on his account. With his "anthropological turn" in talking about God, he led theology into a critical and productive discussion with the spirit of modernity as hardly any one before him had.

Rahner is a classic of modern critical theology, which means he is someone from whom one can still learn even if one has already begun to question and disagree with him. I know whereof I speak. I began questioning and arguing about his view of the philosophical grounding for this "anthropological turn" in Christian talk about God. This turn cannot, in my opinion, be carried out purely in light of the preconditions of consciousness, namely, the transcendental. Rather, it must from the very beginning proceed with a view to the human person in history and society; it must be dialectical. That is why I have spoken of "political theology" as an approach to fundamental theology.

Forty years ago I published a book called *Theology of the World*.[1] It was in its inception completely imbued with Rahner's universalist *pathos* in speaking about God. Rahner fought against the danger—as do I—of an ecclesiological encryption of God-talk. For him—as for me—the God of the Bible and tradition was not just a church issue but a human issue.[2]

So, what was the view of "the world" in this "theology of the world," which already in that early book was represented as the search for a political theology of the relationship of the church and the world? Even then, it was not about the world or human-kind in their abstract, quasi-ahistorical universality, but rather about the world in its concrete historical singularity, about the world in its public historical situation as it breaks into the suppos-edly self-contained world of private faith and tests its hope (see 1 Pet 3:15). "Deprivatization" of the language of faith was the early catchphrase for this attempt at a new political theology.[3] I want to theologically and biographically[4] elaborate a few of those expe-riences of interruption upon which and for which this theology "facing the world" seeks to establish itself as a theological part of the church's storeroom of memories. And so these sketches have a systematic rather than a genealogical intent.

---

1. See Metz, *Theology of the World*. The chapters were previously published from 1962 to 1968.

2. Metz, "Natürliche Gotteskompetenz," in *Memoria Passionia*, 108–22.

3. For a historical clarification of this concept, see my explanation under "Zweierlei Politische Theologie," in *Memoria Passionis*, 252–57.

4. Theology cannot be correctly understood without biography. This marks it off from religious studies and from the philosophy of religion. The theological point is not the biographical dissemination of a personal life story, but rather is the overcoming of today's heightened dualism between the story of faith and life story, between creed and experience. See, e.g., my reflections in the section "Theology as Biography?," in Metz, *Faith in History and Society*, 198–297. This text goes back to my *Laudatio* on the occasion of Karl Rahner's seventieth birthday; it was first published under the title "Karl Rahner—ein theologisches Leben."

The World of War: World War II

Too many dying, too many young men dead for one sixteen-year-old pressed into the military at the end of this war. This biographical background, with which I have burdened my students and which I have publicly discussed in detail, still sets the tone for my theological work. In my theology, for example, present danger plays a central role. This theology does not want to let go of the apocalyptic metaphors of its religious tradition; it mistrusts most of all a flattened out eschatology devoid of all dangers. In this theology, biblical apocalyptic is not at its core nurtured by any frivolous or zealous fantasy of destruction, but rather by a perception of the world that peels back the cover and reveals, unadorned and without illusion, what really is happening, what really is the case. Thus, this theology works against the constant tendency of all religious worldviews to mythically or metaphysically camouflage the horrific disasters in the world and also works against a speculative retouching and an idealistic smoothing out of the actual course of history in order finally to make the victims invisible and their screams inaudible. But to talk about the God of the biblical tradition means to give a memory to those cries and to give time its temporality, its limit.[5]

Let me add this clarification in more academic language: through the years, an increasing sensitivity to theodicy runs through my theological work; that is, there is a growing awareness that to speak of the God of the biblical traditions is to speak in the face of the abysmal history of suffering in the world—in God's world. How can one, in the face of this history of suffering, blithely ask only about one's own salvation? Early on I recognized that whoever talks of God the way Jesus does accepts the violation of preconceived religious certainty by the horrendous tragedy of others. At the root of Christian theology there always lies a matter of justice, the question of justice for those who suffer, of unjust and innocent suffering. *Deus caritas est—Deus iustitia est.* For this reason, Christianity is committed not to a faceless,

---

5. On this, see the section on cultural amnesia in Metz, *Memoria Passionis*, 123–57.

quasi-innocent inner piety, but to a face-seeking "mysticism with eyes open"—which I will discuss later. The biblical monotheistic talk of God can only be universal, can only be meaningful, for all humankind, if it awakens our sensitivity and responsibility to the suffering of others, as Jesus' apocalyptic parable of the Last Judgment (Matt 25:31–46) makes clear.

Thus, in the end I have sought to expand the notion of *memoria passionis*, originally reserved only for Christology within systematic theology, to Christian speech about God overall. In this *memoria passionis*, remembrance of the God of the Bible and church tradition opens itself up to the passion and suffering of humankind, and thereby for that one greatest story, the sole grand narrative that still remains for us after the Enlightenment critique of religion and ideology, after Marxism, and after Nietzsche and the postmodern fragmentation of history: reading the world as in fact the history of human suffering.

The World "After Auschwitz"

I must admit it was not theology but the today-much-maligned atmosphere of 1968 that dispossessed me of an all-too-glib theological discourse about a general historicity of the Christian faith and that forced the *logos* of theology to confront concrete history itself, that public history that bears so catastrophic a name as Auschwitz.

Auschwitz: Has this name become indispensable in theological discussion about God? Or have we once again made this place into no place at all—with the help of a faceless, idealist history empty of a humanity that clothes itself in great apathy in the face of the catastrophes and disasters in this history? But are not we Christians pointed toward that very history by the canon of our faith and our liturgy, by the center of our creed—"suffered under Pontius Pilate," "on the night on which he was betrayed"—toward that history in which there is crucifixion, torture, mourning, love, and hatred? And no ahistorical myth, no Platonic ideal of God, no gnostic doctrine of salvation with its dualistic talk of history without salvation and salvation without history, no abstract talk of the historicity of our existence can restore to us the innocence we have lost in that history.

Certainly for many, also for many Christians, Auschwitz has long ago sunk beneath the horizon of their memory. We have scarcely connected the present crises of humanity and Auschwitz: for instance, the growing deafness vis-à-vis universal and high expectations and judgments, the postmodern compartmentalization, the decline of solidarity, the growing refusal even to include moral perspectives in the notion of a human being, and so on. But are not all of these symptoms a vote of no confidence in humankind? Therefore the question after Auschwitz is not only, Where was God in Auschwitz? but also, Where was humankind in Auschwitz? Looking at the victim forces us also to look at the perpetrator and at the abysmal image of the human being emerging here. In this situation after Auschwitz, I was especially troubled by the despair of those who have survived this catastrophe: so much silent unhappiness, so many suicides! Many have perished out of despair for humanity. Auschwitz has profoundly lowered the metaphysical boundary of shame between human beings. Only the forgetful can survive this—or those who have already successfully forgotten that they have forgotten something. But they too do not escape: one cannot willfully sin even in the name of humanity without betraying the distinction between good and bad.

What would happen if one day people could only defend themselves against misfortune and immorality in the world by using the weapon of forgetfulness? What would happen if one day human beings could only build their happiness on a lack of compassion that forgets the victims, on a culture of amnesia in which supposedly time heals all wounds? What then would nurture the revolt against the senselessness of unjust and innocent suffering in the world? What then would inspire attention to the suffering of others and to the vision of a new, more profound justice? What would then remain if such a cultural amnesia were to come to pass among humankind? What then? A humanity that is "beyond good and evil"? What would happen if the public use of reason no longer provoked the interruption of a rationality guided by forgetfulness? If our modern rationality would no longer permit a categorical imperative that demands of us action that permanently bans the repetition of a catastrophe such as Auschwitz?

The World of the World Church

The first years of my theological post at the University of Münster fell during the time of the Second Vatican Council. Until then, in theology "the world" was formulated and discussed, if at all, in mostly Eurocentric terms. But at the council, the church presented itself for the first time not only dogmatically and intentionally but empirically and in fact as a world church. The non-European world made its first entry into the concrete worldview of the church and her theology. But the world this world church engages is first and foremost a social world torn apart by suffering, and it is a culturally polycentric world. As such, this world becomes a challenge to the universalism of the biblically grounded way of speaking about God. This is yet to be discussed in detail. For now, only the following points can be made. Through countless public debates about God and the world, especially through the Christian-Marxist dialogue in what was called the *Paulus-Gesellschaft* (brought to an abrupt end by the 1968 Russian invasion of Prague), I was sensitized to a new world situation. I understood the debate with Marxism primarily as a discussion about the socially critical dramatization of the theodicy issue. I did not want to save politics and political culture—as any sort of pragmatism recommends—from the gaze of theodicy. Of course I also wanted to bring into the discussion a position other than that of Marxism: I wanted always and unconditionally to ask about the suffering of others, the suffering even of the enemy, and to ask about the sufferings of the dead, to which no impassioned struggle of the living can reconcile. This mix of politics and theodicy had and has a high price: it subjects this political theology again and again to mockery by every political pragmatist and political utopian, outside and inside Christianity. But how does one ultimately rescue political life from pure political Darwinism without the viewpoint of theodicy? These discussions in any case have sharpened the focus of the world church on the world it encounters.

In this world of the world church there is a history of suffering in society, the suffering of the poor, the oppressed, and the wretched. And there is also a cultural history of suffering in that world, the suffering of otherness and of endangered dignity. The conditions experienced in such a world that directly contradict the gospel—such as degradation, exploitation, racism—demand the formulation of the biblical word of God as dangerous memory, in categories of resistance and liberating transformation. For Christians, this transformation, which in Latin American theology is called liberation, entails recognizing the capacity for guilt in all acting subjects. Such a theory of action does not lead ineluctably to a paralysis of the will to change things and so to the stabilization and legitimation of unjust conditions and structures. It wants only to remove this determination to transform the world as a basis for the hatred and violence of terrorism.[6]

The World in the Storms of Globalization

Whoever understands theology as I do, as speaking of God while facing the world, cannot ignore the challenges of the contemporary processes of globalization. And this globalization is a matter not just of the markets and technology, but also of religions and worldviews. The contemporary world of globalization is in any case also the world of an accelerating and inescapably cross-pollinating pluralism of religious and cultural worlds. So tolerance, dialogue, and discourse are usually recommended. These are certainly important. But are there not also limits to tolerance as well as criteria for dialogue? Are there not in the end mistaken developments, "derailments" (J. Habermas), in a sense "pathologies" (J. Ratzinger) in the area of cultures and

6. On the relationship of political theology to Latin American liberation theology, see my *Zum Begriff der neuen Politischen Theologie,* 209–10, and *Memoria Passionis,* 255. On the debate with my Marxist dialogue partners in the Paulus-Gesellschaft, on the significance of my personal engagement with Ernst Bloch and with the Frankfurt School, above all with Theodor W. Adorno and Jürgen Habermas, for my construction of the intelligible and practical basis for a new political theology, see my "Wie ich mich geändert habe," in *Zum Begriff,* 207–11. See also my *Unterbrechungen.*

religions that need to be resisted, that need to be corrected? Are all religions, as we like to assume these days, really the same? Are they the same in regard to the understanding and praxis of religious free- dom, in regard to positive and negative religious freedom—freedom for religion and freedom from religion?

Taking such questions into account is not a matter of theo- logically denying or discarding pluralism, but of seeking to engage it in a way that is open and reasonable to all. In this irrevocably acknowledged diversity of religions and worldviews, is there, how- ever, a criterion for understanding and living together that applies to everyone and is therefore universal and capable of truth? In the end, these questions are not only about the pluralism of religions but also increasingly about the pluralism of forms of life, whether characterized as religious or strictly secular. To this end, I have tentatively suggested a global program for Christianity under the heading of compassion—which I understand not as a somewhat vague empathy, not as an inconsequential pity, not as a philan- thropic sentiment, but as a participatory awareness of the strang- ers' suffering, as an active remembrancing (*Eingedenken*) of the suffering other.[7] Here I can only mention the biblical background. It is important on the one hand that talk of the God of Abraham, Isaac, and Jacob, who is also the God of Jesus, not be misunder- stood as an expression of some sort of abstract, metahistorical monotheism. God-talk is sensitive to suffering at its core. For that reason, in the religious dialogue with Islam, the justifiable link to common biblical roots for talking about God should not lead us to ask about the profound differences in the understanding of Holy Scripture and of monotheism. The understanding of biblical monotheism as fundamentally talk about God that is sensitive to suffering has a reflexive character: it comes from a hermeneutical culture interacting with the Bible as God's word. Can and might

7. For the structural difference between this compassion and the theme of empathy in Eastern traditions, especially Buddhism, see my more detailed ob- servations in "Weltprogram des Christentums im Pluralismus der Religionen und Kulturen" in *Memoria Passionis*, 158–84, also 105–7. On the relationship of compassion to the *logos* of Christian theo-*logy* and its practical foundation, see in addition the remarks that follow these sections, especially 215–57.

there be in Islam—at least at this point—such a hermeneutical approach in engaging the Qur'an?

On the other hand, it is important for the New Testament background of compassion that the messianic Jesus looked first not to the sin, but to the suffering of others.[8] This fundamental sensitivity for others' suffering is exactly what characterized Jesus' new way of life. It has nothing to do with self-pity, nothing to do with a depressive cult of suffering. It is rather the completely unsentimental expression of love, the love that Jesus meant when he spoke—completely in line with his Jewish heritage—of the inseparable unity of love of God and love of neighbor: it is the passion for God as the passion for involvement, as the mysticism of compassion. A Christianity that holds on to its roots in the face of the new dramatic pluralism of religions and cultures is ever and again about this union. In my view, this passion for involvement may be considered the dowry of Christianity, its world program for the age of globalization.

Since this world program seeks to speak to and invite all human beings, religious as well as secular, I have to at least mention the concept of reason in this theology that suggests such a world program. Reason in this theology is not seen as morally indifferent. Remembrance of others' suffering is intrinsic to reason and guarantees its human character. Hence this *logos* contradicts a rationality that is tied primarily to safeguarding its universal validity and efficacy above or outside the concrete historical and moral world. In such talk about the human, any sense of connection between historical origin and normative validity falls out of the picture. This disconnect touches on a central problem of modern rationality and its anthropology.

---

8. This reference is not meant to play the sensitivity to suffering demanded by Christianity off against its basic sensitivity to sin. Here it is asked with a corrective intent whether the equally fundamental sensitivity to suffering in Christianity has not been overshadowed by the necessary, but one-sided, emphasis on sensitivity to sin against ourselves and above all against others and against the world. On the fundamental question of the extent to which the theological turn in Christianity has given rise to a tendency to ignore the question of those who suffer with its related theme of theodicy and to formulate Christology exclusively as soteriology, see Metz, *Memoria Passionis*, 50–62 and 163–66.

In no way do I now want to join those who claim to have overcome the Enlightenment without having passed through it. Where modern reasoning tries, in the name of the Enlightenment, to completely distance itself from the historical dialectic between remembering and forgetting, where it actually abandons the "dialectic of the Enlightenment" for the benefit of purely rational discourse, it inevitably grounds the process of enlightenment in forgetfulness and thereby stabilizes the prevailing cultural amnesia with its extremely feeble awareness of what is missing.[9]

In the present dispute over the "human experiment," modern rationality can ensure its humane character over against the increasing dominance of technical rationality only by talking about the human being within a memory-laden semantic, a memory already embedded in our human language itself—and so based not simply on a natural development, but rather on a historical background. The human being—as known and entrusted to us until now—is more than its own experiment: it is also—and fundamentally—its own memory. Human beings are a result not only of their genes but also of their histories. If they want to understand who they are, humans need not only to experiment with themselves but also to allow themselves to be told something. For that reason, the distinction suggested here between technical and anamnestic reason is important not only for theology but also for anthropology; and in any case, it is important if the human being is to be and to remain more than a bit of nature in a last unfinished experiment in biotechnology or neurotechnology.

I return to *compassion*. Compassion is not only for our private lives but also for our public, political lives. It sends us to the front of today's political, social, and cultural conflicts. At least the spirit of compassion holds out an offer of peace for our globalized world. Only this sort of "suffering with" breaks the power of, for example, that basic enmity that dominates the Near East. Only if some ethic of compassion breaks into political conflicts, only if the memory of the suffering of one's own people is also bound up with a willingness

9. For general remarks on the dialectical character of anamnestic reason, see Metz, *Memoria Passionis*, 215–57.

not to forget the suffering of others, even the suffering of former enemies, and to take into account this history of the other's suffering in future negotiations will there be new paths to peace.

In the end, what really does prevent our globalized world from imploding into uncontrolled religious and cultural wars: here Christianity, there Islam; here the West, there the Arab world? What is there in this era of globalization that can hold our world together in peace? It is the proposition that human beings are fundamentally equal, that the strongest of assumptions about humanity has a biblical foundation. Expressed in the moral language adopted by Christianity and proclaimed by the message of the inseparable unity of love of God and love of neighbor, of a passion for God and a passion for compassion, it goes something like this: there is no suffering in the world that does not concern us. This principle of the fundamental equality of all human beings entails the recognition of an authority that is open to and reasonable for all people: the authority of those who suffer, of the victims of unjust and innocent suffering, an authority that, prior to any consent or agreement, places a claim on all human beings—yes, on *all* people, whether religious or secular—and therefore cannot be relativized or avoided by any humane culture that insists on the equality of all humans, or by any religion, not even by the church. For this reason also the recognition of this authority would be the criterion by which to orient religious and cultural discourse in a globalized context. Finally it would be the basis of an ethic of peace for a truly pluralistic world. In any case, a European politics and ultimately a global politics that knows itself to be bound to this biblical heritage of compassion would be something other than the agent of the market and technology and their supposedly practical constraints in the era of globalization.

Conclusion

These are a few sketches from my many years of theological work. Over the course of time I have increasingly moved away from talking about God and his Christ in a way that is subjectless and historically untethered. Thus, for me, theology has become more bound to the world and in this sense more political. With this willingness to risk engaging history, the history of the suffering of humankind forces its way into theological discourse about the salvation history of humankind. Theology expresses itself not only in singing, but also in crying out. Certainly Christians are mystics but, in distinction to the mysticism of the Far East, Christians are mystics with open eyes, mystics of a compassion, of a willingness to suffer with others, which has become an important watchword for the praxis of the discipleship of Jesus, a praxis without which Christian theology cannot remain true to its *logos*. This mysticism of compassion is no faceless mysticism of suffering as in the main forms of Eastern mysticism.[10] Rather, it is much more a face-seeking mysticism. It leads us to encounter the face of the suffering other. This defining experience is not just secular, but an earthly glimpse of the closeness of God in his Christ: "'Lord, when did we see you suffering?' And he answered them: 'Truly, I say to you, whatever you have done for one of these little ones, you have done for me. Whatever you have not done for these little ones, you have not done for me!'" (Matt 25:39-40). So I hope that in these sketches I have not been talking about "my" theology, but simply about a piece of theology from the storeroom of Christian memory.

Translated by John K. Downey

10. In this Eastern mysticism of suffering, it is the experience of the opposition between the self (the "I") and the world that generates suffering and that needs to be overcome. The "I" of human beings needs to be seen through as an "illusion" (Nietzsche: "as a projection") and at the end of a long process should dissolve into the faceless unity and harmony of the universe. To the extent that this "I" has a mystical character, the basis for the experience of compassion is absent. What the New Testament calls "dying to oneself" begins with our relativizing our own preconceived wishes and interests in the readiness to allow ourselves to be interrupted by the suffering of others. One thinks of the well-known parable of the "merciful Samaritan" with which Jesus has captured not only the remembrance of Christianity but also the remembrance of humanity.

CHAPTER 2

God and the Evil of This World

Forgotten, Unforgettable Theodicy

THE TOPIC OF THIS issue, "The Return of the Plague," finally confronts theology with the question which in scholastic terminology is discussed under the heading of theodicy. How does talk of God—note, not some postmodern invented "God," but the remembered God of the biblical traditions, of the God of Abraham, Isaac, and Jacob who is also the God of Jesus—relate to the experiences of evil, suffering, and wickedness in the world, in "his" world? Attempts at such a theological answer, a theological explanation of evil in the world, have been and are manifold. They cannot be pursued in detail within the framework of this text, nor should they be[1]—especially as my starting point is that there is no "answer," no "solution," to this question by means of which theology could settle it once and for all, provided that the question is put properly. This conclusion governs my approach. But anyone who speaks of God in the sense of the biblical traditions encounters the question of theodicy. It is and remains *the* eschatological question. What does it mean?

---

1. In his brief work, "Why Does God Let Us Suffer?" Karl Rahner offers a brief but convincing criticism of the common attempts to make sense of the suffering and evil of this world.

Exodus Theodicy—Job Theodicy

This issue of *Concilium* picks up a word that is familiar to us from the biblical traditions, the so-called "plagues of Egypt." In the book of Exodus, these plagues are described in detail and a "justification" is also given for this visitation of misery on Egypt. This is a divine punitive action against the Pharaoh of Egypt with his sinfully hardened heart, who is preventing the liberating exodus of Israel. Evil as a punishment for sin: down to the present day, this is a recurrent motif in "answers" to the question of theodicy. However, already in the biblical traditions themselves there is a counter-story to this Exodus theodicy, namely the Job theodicy. This Job theodicy makes it quite clear (and in the relevant narrative passages even finds the approval of God himself for this) that the plagues which fall on Job, his suffering and his misfortune, have nothing to do with his sin or with his failure before God. Here a just and innocent man is suffering! So there is no causal connection between suffering and sin.

The Eschatological Question

In order to take account of the complexity of the theodicy question, I do not propose to start directly from the "plagues," from the evils of this world, but from what I would like to call here the "human history of suffering."[2] In my view, this category of the history of suffering undermines the familiar distinction between physical evils (natural catastrophes, epidemics, illnesses . . .) and "moral evil" (guilt, evil); however, above all it prevents an over-hasty ontologizing of the problem, of the kind known to us from the history of theology and philosophy, especially in all dualistic or quasi-dualistic attempts at an explanation, that is, in the theodicy of Gnosticism and the Gnostic relapse in Christianity.[3] Now if we

2. For this encounter see my text "Suffering unto God," 611–22.

3. See here, for example, the investigations by H. Blumenberg in *Säkularisierung*. Theodor W. Adorno has pointed out that concepts of theodicy, which make use of an ontological argument and end up in an ontology of

begin with the "human history of suffering," we shall no longer misunderstand theodicy as the attempt at a belated and to some degree defiant "justification of God" by theology in the face of the evil, suffering, and wickedness in the world. Moreover, we shall recognize that theodicy is concerned, indeed is exclusively concerned, with the question of how it is possible to talk of God at all in the face of the abysmal history of suffering in a world which we acknowledge in faith to be God's creation. This question may not be either eliminated or over-answered by theology; it is, as I have already said, *the* eschatological question. Theology does not work out any all-reconciling answer to it but continually seeks a new language and *praxis* in order to make it unforgettable.

Two Fundamental Reservations

Of course there are objections to such a "weak" conception of theodicy. Here I shall discuss—briefly—two fundamental reservations, namely (1) objections which are made in the name of reason and (2) objections which are made in the name of Christian doctrine.

1. Does not this conception contradict a principle of human reason which is expressed, for example, in Occam's razor; *entia sine ratione non sunt multiplicanda* (entities are not to be multiplied without reason)? Applied to our topic, is it not necessary on rational grounds finally to drop and forget a question to which, it is granted, there can be no answer? But what if one day human beings could defend themselves against the unhappiness in the world only with the weapon of forgetfulness, if they could build their happiness only on the uncompassionate forgetfulness of the victims, on a culture of amnesia? What if only time heals all wounds (and one day even the wounds which bear the name of Auschwitz)? If that happens, on what does resistance to the senselessness of suffering in the world feed? What inspires an attentiveness to

---

the torment of creation. See also J.A. Zamora's work on Adorno, *Krise, Kritik, Erinnerung.*

the suffering of others and the vision of a new and greater justice? What remains if this cultural amnesia is complete? The human being? What human being? An appeal to the self-preservation of the human in this instance seems to me to be highly abstract. It derives not least from an anthropology which has long bidden farewell to the question of evil and the "perspective of theodicy" in human history and which forgets that not only the individual human being but also the "idea" of humanity is vulnerable, indeed can be destroyed.

2. Does not the "weak" conception of theodicy presented here contradict the theological understanding of Christianity as this has developed over centuries? Is not Christianity the successful response to and also the stilling of that question of theodicy which accompanied the history of the faith of Israel in the form of lament, cry, and insatiable expectation—in the Psalms, in Job, in Lamentations, in many passages in the prophetic books? Is not Christology, is not above all Christian soteriology, the answer to the question of the history of human suffering in God's good creation?[4]

But even the Christology of Christians does not lack eschatological unrest. Not only Israel has constantly moved in an eschatological "landscape of cries"[5]; as is well known, the New Testament, the biography of early Christianity, ends with a cry, with a cry which now has a Christological point, though in the meantime this has usually been silenced in a mythical or idealist-hermeneutical way. In his article, "Why Does God Let Us Suffer?"[6] Karl Rahner mentions an account by Walter Dirks which has often been quoted since, of a meeting with Romano Guardini, who already had the marks of death on him. This is an account in which it becomes

---

4. For the aporias of the classical position of Augustine and contemporary attempts to respond to the question of theodicy with talk of the "suffering God," see all the contributions in my edited volume *"Landschaft aus Schreien."* See also Gross and Kuschel, *"Ich schaffe Finsternis und Heil."*

5. A formulation of Nelly Sachs.

6. See note 1 above.

dramatically clear how much the question of theodicy constantly disturbs the whole of Christian doctrine:

> The one who experiences it will not forget what the old man on his sick bed entrusted to him. He would not only allow himself to be asked questions at the Last Judgement but would also himself ask questions: he confidently hopes that the angel would not refuse to give him a true answer to the question which no book, not even scripture, no dogma and no magisterium, no "theodicy" and theology, not even his own, has been able to answer for him, "Why, God, this fearful way round to salvation, the suffering of the innocent, guilt?"[7]

Why the burden and excessive demands of the human history of suffering? Why guilt? This question remains. Why sin? This "first" question of theodicy does not derive from a typically intellectual cult of questioning, which would indeed be most remote from the sufferers themselves. No vague speculative questions, but passionate personal questions are part of that experience of God about which Christians have had to learn time and again. And this above all because the mysticism which Jesus lived and taught is not really a mysticism of closed eyes but a mysticism of open eyes, which obligates us to a heightened perception of the suffering of others.

Jesus' First Gaze

Christianity began as a community which remembered and told stories in the footsteps of Jesus, whose first gaze was not directed to the sin of others but to the suffering of others. This sensitivity to the suffering of others, this heeding of the suffering of others—including the suffering of enemies—in Jesus' own action lies at the center of that "new way of living" which is associated with him. It is the most convincing expression of that love which Jesus entrusted to us and asked of us when—completely in line

---

7. Rahner, "Why Does God Let Us Suffer?," 207–8.

with his Jewish heritage—he invoked the unity of love of God and love of neighbor.

There are parables of Jesus with which he told himself into human memory. One of the best-known parables is that of the "Good Samaritan," with which he illustrates this love. Here (in the imagery of an archaic provincial society) it is the one who fell among thieves who is disregarded by the priest and the Levite "in the interest of higher things." Those who look for "God" as Jesus understands God do not know "any higher interest" to excuse them here. This authority of the sufferer is the only authority in which the authority of the God who judges manifests itself in the world for all human beings (Matt 25:31–46). Conscience constitutes itself in obedience to it, and what we call its voice is our reaction to a visitation by this suffering of others.

However, at a very early stage Christianity lost its elemental sensitivity to suffering. The question of justice for innocent sufferers which disturbs the biblical traditions was restated too quickly and transformed into the question of redemption for the guilty. Thus, theology believed that it could draw the sting of the question of theodicy. The question of suffering found itself in a soteriological circle. Christianity transformed itself from a religion which was primarily sensitive to suffering into a religion which was primarily sensitive to sin. The focus of attention was no longer on the suffering of the creature but on its guilt. That paralyzed the elemental sensitivity to the suffering of others and darkened the biblical vision of the great justice of God, though according to Jesus this had to apply to all hunger and thirst.

Questions about the Adventure of Theodicy

Our concern here has been above all with a background reflection on the question of God and the evils of this world, on fate and the enduring significance of the question of theodicy in Christianity. But is not this concentration on the question of theodicy too much characterized by resignation and evasion? Are there any open ears in Christianity to the heightened sensitivity for the suffering of others? Should not religion protect us from the pain of negativity? If it does anything at all, does it not serve the triumph of the "positive," the optimizing of the chances of survival? And finally, is not the sensitivity to suffering addressed here an attitude which is very difficult for young people in particular to achieve and show to others? Youth and theodicy: is not that *a priori* a combination doomed to failure?

I can attempt to answer this only with a counter-question. To whom should one entrust the attention addressed here which is paid to the suffering of others, an attitude of empathy which is boundless ("There is no suffering in the world which does not concern us"[8])? Of whom should one require the adventurous notion of being there for others before one receives anything from them? To whom could one offer the "other way of living" thus indicated? To whom, I ask myself, if not to young people in particular? Have we completely forgotten that Christianity once began as a revolt of the youth within the Jewish world of the time?

Has Christianity possibly already grown too old for the sensitivity to suffering which is required by Jesus? Is the refusal of a theodicy really the sign of a living Christianity? Is it not rather the sign of a Christianity which is growing old? The older Christianity becomes, the more "affirmative" it seems to become, the more closed it seems to be, passing over the refractory features of creation. A sense of the misfortune of others is withering away; the steadfastness of faith is insidiously becoming the steadfastness of bewilderment. Anyone who now still has questions, passionate questions, for God is suspected of either loosing the tongue of doubt or propagating a cult of negativity. For me, the specifically Christian form of fundamentalism is reflected in such an attitude. Such a kind of fundamentalism is a symptom of aging, which does not really dare to look the negative features of the world in the face. It has lost the first gaze of Jesus.

Translated by John Bowden

8. A formulation of Peter Rottländer.

CHAPTER 3

On God and Happiness

Jürgen Manemann[1]: Professor Metz, the mass media constantly point out the connection between religion and happiness. Religious people are supposedly happier than those who are not religious. Does religion make one happy?

JBM: For me it all depends on how one understands "happiness" and "religion." "Happy is he who forgets what can no longer be changed." This sentence from *Der Vogelhändler* is a sort of folk wisdom. For religious people this proposition is quite dubious, at least for those for whom being religious has something to do with God, is founded on God. Where there is no God, the ability to forget may be the sole condition for untroubled happiness. Where belief in God is bound up with the biblical names Abraham, Isaac, and Jacob, those who believe in the God of Jesus accept that the misfortune of others may violate their own preconceived desires and dreams of happiness. I take this for example as the key message of some of the Jesus' parables, those parables with which he has talked himself not just into the memory of the church but into the memory of humankind.

Manemann: Can one say then that Jesus was happy with his father?

---

1. Interview conducted by Jürgen Manemann, Professor of Religion, Culture, and Christianity on the Catholic Faculty of the University of Erfurt (Metz, "On God and Happiness," 124–25).

JBM: I have often asked myself this question. My answer has often been discussed and it was not always accepted by everyone. One thing seems clear to me: the life story of Jesus is focused on the story of his passion and not on the story of a happy victor. The situation seems clear: there is a son who from his perspective never abandoned his father but who feels himself abandoned by this father at the end. "My God, my God, why have you forsaken me?" Yet there is a son who, in this experience of God's abandonment, does not despair. Should we call him happy because of this? Happiness here is understood in the common usage. We aren't allowed to define happiness in a way no one uses it today just so that it fits Jesus. We must take into account the ordinary semantics of happiness; otherwise, talking about happiness in this connection doesn't make much sense. And so I would answer: no, one cannot really say that Jesus was happy with his father. I would even say that, in principle, if one thinks about Jesus and his life story, it is nowhere clearer than here that happiness—as that word is ordinarily used—is very important in human relations, but strictly speaking it is hardly a category for the divine-human relationship. Biblically inspired religion—unless it is piously deceiving itself—is not easy. And the biblical proclamation of the unity of the love of God and the love of neighbor, which commits Christians to experiencing God not with their eyes closed but with their eyes open, does not, in my opinion, primarily promote our familiar feeling of happiness but rather questions whether our passion for God is really *compassion.* Whoever wants to call this an experience of happiness may do so, but it would be a conception of happiness at a higher level.

Manemann: The biblical evidence seems to confirm your position considering that the Greek word for happiness, eudaimonia, *doesn't appear in the biblical texts.*

JBM: Possibly because this Greek *eudemonia* indicates too much a "happiness" oriented to personal identity, a happiness too self-satisfied, too steeped in itself. The people of the Bible—as I understand it—always have one question or cry too many, beyond what would allow them to be free of longing. They do not know happiness without longing. For that reason, the biblical Israel—to use a phrase from Nelly Sachs which I like very much—finally always appears as a "landscape of cries." And the New Testament, the first biography of Christianity, also ends with a cry, with a now Christologically sharpened cry: "*Maranatha.*" If one wants to call that being happy. . . .

Manemann: "All human beings strive for happiness." One finds this proposition in Aristotle as well as Augustine, Aquinas, Kant, and others. What meaning does this phrase have for you?

JBM: I can agree with this statement if a categorical imperative derived from this one common striving for happiness goes something like: strive for happiness but not at the cost of the happiness of others.

Manemann: The Declaration of Independence of the United States of America speaks of the right to happiness. What do you think of this claim? Is there a right to happiness? And is there something like a politics of happiness?

JBM: I would answer in exactly the same way: that claim reminds our seemingly innate individual striving for happiness to always remember the misfortune of others. In this sense, the right to happiness proclaimed here speaks simultaneously of a duty: the duty of the happy to the unhappy. So understood, this right belongs to the foundations of the common good, and in this sense it would also be the foundation for an ambitious politics of happiness.

Translated by John K. Downey

Part II

Remembering Suffering

CHAPTER 4

Between Remembering and Forgetting

The Shoah in the Era of Cultural Amnesia

I.

I BELONG TO THAT generation of Germans who slowly, much too slowly, learned to understand themselves as a generation "after Auschwitz," and I sought in my way of doing theology to do justice to this understanding, insofar as possible. Auschwitz signaled for me a terror beyond all familiar theology, a terror that left any non-contextual talk of God empty and blind. I asked myself: With such a catastrophe at one's back, is there a God to whom one can pray? Can any theology worthy of its name simply continue to speak, continue to speak of God and human beings, as if in the face of such a catastrophe one must not scrutinize the assumed innocence of our human words? My intention with such questions is not to stylize Auschwitz into a negative myth that would again remove this catastrophe from our theological and historical purview. First and foremost, it was all about the unsettling question: Why is this catastrophe—as with the history of human suffering itself—so little, or even not at all, apparent in the words and images of theology? The noticeably apathetic content of Christian theology, its astounding resistance to being disconcerted in the face of the Shoah, upset me. From that point on, I have attempted to do Christian theology with full consciousness of the situation "after Auschwitz." My purpose, however, is not to give this catastrophe a Christian meaning, let alone a Christian "reception," but rather to do "theology after Auschwitz" primarily as critique of theology.

II.

"The Shoah between Remembering and Forgetting." With this theme, I am addressing not only theology, but the "very spirit (*geistige Situation*) of our time" (K. Jaspers). In my opinion, there has been in this regard a momentous shift or a change of mentalities. In sum, I could say, the mystery of redemption is no longer called remembrance, but rather forgetting. We are living more and more in an era of cultural amnesia.

Under the title of postmodernity are we not slipping increasingly into a world that cultivates forgetting? Human beings are less and less their own memories, ever more only their own unlimited experiments. Friedrich Nietzsche, who as the presence behind the spirit of our times has long supplanted Hegel and Marx, connected his "new way to live," with which he tried to do away with Christianity and all monotheistic religion, with the triumph of cultural amnesia.

> In the smallest and greatest happiness there is always one thing that makes it happiness: the power of forgetting . . . . One who cannot leave himself behind on the threshold of the moment and forget the past, who cannot stand on a single point, like a goddess of victory, without fear or giddiness, will never know what happiness is.[1]

The vision of human happiness is grounded now very simply in the capacity to forget, in the amnesia of the victor or at least the one who has made it through. "Blessed are the forgetful,"[2] declares Nietzsche, and juxtaposes his "beatitude" with that of Jesus of Nazareth: "Blessed are those who mourn," those who cannot overcome the pain of remembrance.

1. Nietzsche, *Use and Abuse of History*, 6.
2. Nietzsche, "Beyond Good and Evil," 217, in *Basic Writings*, 336.

But how can this be true? Isn't there enough talk of the past and of overcoming the past in Germany? Of the Historians' Controversy and its consequences? Isn't our public domain characterized by discussions about "monuments of warning," about Holocaust memorials, by controversies about the Armed Forces exhibition in Germany and Austria, and about Daniel Goldhagen's book *Hitler's Willing Executioners*? Where is the predominance of forgetting, the era of cultural amnesia in which we are supposedly living? Let us see!

In my estimation, the totally networked information society that we are becoming cannot resist this forgetting. On the contrary, this society is in danger of becoming a "forgetting machine" because storing information is, in fact, not remembering. In the words of H. M. Enzensberger: "Storing—that means forgetting."[3] To get to the bottom of our question, I would like to quote Nietzsche again, Nietzsche in his entire ambivalence, Nietzsche who was not at all the blind fanatic of forgetting. In his thoughts in *The Genealogy of Morals*, he writes,

> How can one create a memory for the human animal?
> How can one impress something upon this partly obtuse,
> partly flighty mind, attuned only to the passing moment,
> in such a way that it will stay there? . . . If something is to
> stay in the memory, it must be burned in: only that which
> never ceases to *hurt* stays in memory.[4]

Cultural amnesia means shutting down the pain of remembrance in the cultural memory of human beings. Jean-François Lyotard rightly emphasizes that there are actually two kinds of forgetting. On the one hand, there is the destruction of all evidence, so that there is nothing more to remember (as the Nazis tried to do with the death chambers). On the other hand, there is also the "perfect" memory, namely, the presumed certainty

---

3. Enzensberger, "Gedankenflucht (1)," *Kiosk*, 31: "Stored, that means forgotten." Formerly I used an opposite formulation that nonetheless makes the same point: "The computer cannot remember because it cannot forget anything."

4. Nietzsche, "On the Genealogy of Morals," II.3, in *Basic Writings*, 497.

that the event in and with its (later) representation has been preserved and understood.[5]

III.

The contemporary triumph of amnesia rests on different foundations.

1. The first, in my opinion, is Christian theology itself. Has it not always used much too strong categories for its perception of history, categories that all too quickly cover up all the historical injuries, all the gaping wounds, all the collapses and catastrophes, and that spare the talk of God from the pain of remembering? Must not the Shoa, at least, work as an ultimatum to an all-too-easy theological intercourse with history? Must not, in any case, the question of the locus and the degree of the horror turn up in the midst of the *logos* of theology? Must not theology, in any case, now be convinced that it does not heal all wounds?

   The evidence of cultural amnesia in Christian theology reaches far into the past—back to the history of its separation from Jewish tradition. Very early on, Christianity deployed a questionable and momentous strategy of an institutional and intellectual disinheritance vis-à-vis Judaism. On the one hand, Christianity understood itself as the new Israel, as the new Jerusalem, as the true people of God. The originating importance of Israel for Christians, as Paul urgently warns in his Letter to the Romans, was too quickly displaced: Israel was demoted to an obsolete precondition for Christianity in the scheme of salvation history. At the same time, there began what I call the "halving" of the Christian spirit, as Christianity became theologized. The faith tradition of Israel was ostensibly invoked, but the spirit was taken exclusively from Athens, more precisely from the Hellenistic tradition. In other words, from a subjectless and

5. See Bernhardt, "Die Kehrseite," 931.

ahistorical thought structure of Being and Identity, in which ideas are always more foundational than memories and time knows no boundaries. Athens vs. Jerusalem? Didn't Jerusalem, didn't the biblical Jewish traditions and Jewish experience of the postbiblical era, didn't Jewish thought right up to our time offer any specific intellectual paradigms? Naturally, these Jewish intellectual paradigms exist. There is thinking as "being mindful of" (*Eingedenken*), there is that anamnestic culture that does not spare itself the pain of remembering and which knows that not time, but rather the eschatological God, heals wounds, if they are healed at all.

2. Certainly modern science does not break the spell of the cultural amnesia that I have described. In our civilization, science is the paradigm of normality, and thus one can say of science that it heals all wounds and does not know the pain of remembering. I would like to make a special remark regarding the human sciences. As I see it, since the German Historians' Controversy (*Deutscher Historikerstreit*, 1986–88), the historicization of National Socialism and its crimes has more or less come to be the prevailing view in the human sciences.[6] Regarding Auschwitz, the question remains for me of how a terror that repeatedly threatens to remove itself from historical consciousness can nonetheless be kept in memory. This can only be accomplished by a historiography that is supported by an anamnestic culture, by a memorial culture that knows about the sort of forgetting that is still ingrained in every historicized objectivization.

6. M. Broszat, who recommends and defends the concept of historicization, does not understand it in the sense of memory-distant "removal" of the German past (*Entsorgung der Vergangenheit*). "Whoever wishes to talk the citizens of the German Federal Republic out of their self-critical consideration of their older and more recent history, robs them of one of the best elements of the political culture that has slowly developed since the late fifties in this nation. What is most treacherous in this regard is the fundamental misconception that the moral sensibility vis-à-vis their own history achieved through necessity was a cultural and political disadvantage compared with other nations."

For the most part, we are deprived of such a culture in Europe because we lack the spirit that Auschwitz was supposed to extinguish once and for all. In the last analysis, it is the Jewish spirit that is the privileged carrier of such an anamnestic culture. Therefore, I tend to speak of a double-destruction, a double-death, so to speak, in the Shoah. Not only were the Jews murdered with technical-industrial perfection; with them that very spirit was supposed to be extinguished, and once and for all destroyed, that makes us capable of remembering this unimaginable horror and keeping it present in memory: the anamnestic culture of the human spirit itself. Over and over again I have asked myself whether we deal so ambivalently and uncertainly with Auschwitz because we lack the anamnestic spirit that would be necessary to perceive and express appropriately what also happened to us, to what we call spirit, in this catastrophe. In short, whether we deal ambivalently with Auschwitz because we lack a memorial culture that is more deeply rooted than our scientific perception of history and that knows the pain of memory.

3. "Science heals all wounds." Doesn't this also apply to the major and influential portion of contemporary philosophy? In a text entitled "Israel and Athens: or, To Whom Does Anamnestic Reason Belong?" the famous German philosopher Jürgen Habermas tried to make clear that the anamnestic spirit of biblical thought has long since penetrated European philosophical reason.[7] Why then, for example, in Habermas's work itself, does the catastrophe of Auschwitz appear in his *Minor Political Works*—and there, as is known, quite clearly and in a very influential and convincing fashion—but with not even a single word in his major philosophical writings concerning communicative reason? Does the theory of communicative competence, perhaps, also heal all wounds? How then would one speak in a generalizable fashion of what remains a disaster, of what cannot be healed, of what cannot

7. Habermas, "Israel und Athen," 51–64.

be allowed to disappear behind the curtain of cultural amnesia, of what does not allow itself to be shut away behind an impervious wall of normality? How could one speak of that which demands, when at all, another kind of forgiveness than the forgiveness of time that supposedly heals everything, or than the forgiveness of theory that closes all wounds?

IV.

Nonetheless, there is something remaining even when all wounds have seemingly been closed. What remains is hard to describe. It is an unusual feeling of something missing that resists the complete assuaging of the pain of remembering, whether purely theoretically, psychologically, aesthetically, in rituals of memory, or even religiously. What is it? This something missing in the present is least understood when it is ascribed to a typical sensitivity of the older generations, as is most often done. It is much rather the case, in my opinion, that the younger generation exhibits precisely this sense of something missing. It fuels the skepticism of the young, their indifference, at times their anger toward "the" experience, "the" point of view, "the" lesson of history which the older generation has offered them, has imposed on them, and has elevated to the canon of normality. What is most remarkable for me about the recent discussion in Germany of Daniel Goldhagen and his book subtitled *Ordinary Germans and the Holocaust*[8] is that the practically unanimous and—according to the criteria of professional historiography—fully correct critique of the experts has nonetheless failed to soothe the upset of so many younger people over the magnitude of the guilt involved.

Being mindful of the suffering of others remains a fragile category in our time, a time in which human beings in the end are of the opinion that it is only with the sword of forgetting and the shield of amnesia that they can arm themselves against the latest waves of the history of suffering and evil deeds: yesterday,

8. Goldhagen, *Hitler's Willing Executioners.*

Auschwitz; today, Bosnia and Rwanda; and tomorrow? But this forgetting is not without consequences.

For many, Auschwitz has certainly long since disappeared beyond the horizon of their memories. Yet no one can avoid the anonymous consequences. The theological question after Auschwitz is not only: Where was God at Auschwitz? It is also: Where was humankind at Auschwitz?

What has always particularly touched and troubled me about the situation "after Auschwitz" was the affliction, the hopelessness of those who survived this catastrophe—so much silent misery, so many suicides! Clearly these people were shattered by their despair about the human race, about that which human beings are capable of toward one another. This catastrophe vastly lowered the metaphysical and moral threshold of shame among human beings; it injured the bands of solidarity between all those who bear a human face. Only those without memory survive something like this; or those who have already successfully forgotten that they have forgotten something. One cannot sin randomly at the expense of humankind. Not only the individual human being, but also the idea of human beings and of humanity can be injured. Only a few connect the current crisis of humanity with the Shoah, for example, the so-called crisis of values, the increasing deafness to demands for "greatness," the crisis of solidarity, etc. Isn't this all a vote of no-confidence against human beings and their morals?

It is not just the superficial history of the human species that is real; there is also a deep history and it can be wounded through and through. Don't the contemporary orgies of violence and rape reap the benefits of the normative force of the factual? Don't they, behind the mask of amnesia, break down the original trust of civilization, those moral and cultural reserves that ground the humanity of human beings? How exhausted are these reserves? Are we witnessing, perhaps, the end of the paradigm of humanity to which we have been historically accustomed until now? Could it be that human beings in the grip of cultural amnesia have lost not only God, but also, increasingly, themselves, insofar as they have lost what previously was emphatically known as humanity? What remains, therefore, when we have repeatedly successfully closed all wounds? When cultural amnesia is complete? What remains? Human beings? Which human beings? The appeal to humanity is itself highly abstract. It frequently has its source in a naively optimistic anthropology that long ago lost sight of the problem of evil and of a view of human history from the vantage point of theodicy.

In order not to allow the pain of history, the *pathos* of memory, to evaporate in this time of cultural amnesia, we need the power that is the converse of what I have termed anamnestic culture. Religion, in its essence, is characterized by this anamnestic culture. It has its first home in the monotheistic root religion of Judaism. Therefore, the mass murder of the European Jews and Hitler's attempt to annihilate the Jewish people, at least in Europe, can be seen as an unparalleled and unprecedented attack upon the cultural memory of humanity, as the murder of memory on the scale of millions (memory-cide), if this term is appropriate. Nowhere in the world was memory, as religious and cultural force, so fully enfleshed in a human collective as in the Jewish people from Moses to Moses Mendelssohn and beyond.[9]

This resistance to cultural amnesia has allies not only in religion. Religion finds assistance in a body of literature that teaches us to see the panorama of history through the eyes of the victims, and in art that comprehends and expresses itself as the visualization of the memory of the suffering of others. In addition, we should mention here cinematic artworks that call to mind the situation of pain and guilt in a way that the objective lens of scientific historicization cannot achieve. All of these arts have an essence that "carries after." They carry after us, who are enamored of forgetting, the pain of remembering. If we take things very exactly, there is for us no time "after" the Shoah in the way that there can be a time after Hitler and after Stalin.

Translated by Leo J. Penta

9. Weinrich, *Lethe,* 232.

CHAPTER 5

In Memory of the Other's Suffering

Theological Reflections on the Future of Faith and Culture[1]

Memoria Passionis as a Bridge Category between Faith and Culture

CHRISTIAN TALK ABOUT GOD is joined to a very specific kind of memory. I would like to characterize it as a *memoria passionis*. What does this mean? It is evident that the bib lical traditions' way of talking about God is distinguished by a sensitivity to suffering. It is a God-talk that is constitutively "broken" by the theodicy question which remains as unanswerable as it is unforgettable. This God-talk does not have one answer too many, but one question too many for all our answers. It is a way of speaking about God in which history is not simply the history of the victors but above all a history of suffering. It is therefore historically focused on the *memoria passionis* without which the Christian *memoria resurrectionis* would also develop into a pure myth from the side of the victors.

Admittedly, again and again Christian speaking about God took on the trappings of a monotheism marked by the politics of power. This is why it is still under suspicion today as being a source of legitimation for a pre-democratic concept of sovereignty and the source of inspiration for fundamentalisms that are hostile to

---

1. I have further developed the thoughts put forward in this text in "Compassion," 9–18.

pluralism. But talk about the God of Abraham, Isaac, and Jacob—who is also the God of Jesus—is in its core a God-talk that is sensitive to suffering. It is not the expression of just any kind of monotheism but, as one might say, of a monotheism of empathy.

Certainly, this empathetic monotheism is also a kind of universalism. For this monotheism, God is either a theme for all humanity or it is not a theme at all. This God cannot be *my* God if God cannot also at the same time be *your* God. God cannot be *ours* if God cannot also be the God of others, indeed, of all the others. Thus we Christians would turn out, in a certain sense, to be the last universalists in the era of postmodern fragmentations. This is why we shall not give up the "great" themes (about morality and the good, about peace and justice, about religion . . .). But we shall try to speak about them in new ways, with new categories which may sound "weak" or "fragile" in comparison with the familiar ones.

We are living in a world of unfathomable plurality. What is called for, it is said, is tolerance and dialogue or discourse. Is this the answer? Is it enough? Are there not also limits to tolerance and criteria for dialogue? As always, pluralism is not simply the answer, but first of all the question and the problem. To resolve this problem does not mean to dissolve pluralism, but to develop a form of responding to it that is accessible and reasonable to all. In this we seek to avoid a cultural relativism without, however, relativizing the cultures themselves. Yet what then would be this "universal" link—the "universal good" that is mostly denied or at least found missing today, what could be generally accessible and acceptable, that does not relativize cultures but helps constitute them? The taking into memory of alien, foreign suffering, the suffering of the other. How can what we call tolerance avoid cultural relativism? Where are the limits of tolerance? Who defines them and who guarantees them? There is only the resistance of a category that is "weak" in itself, the category of *memoria passionis*.

The biblical traditions to which Christian talk of God is committed know this special form of universal responsibility. One must realize, however, that the universalism of this responsibility is not orientated primarily to the universalism of sin and failure, but to the universalism of suffering in the world. Jesus' first glance was not upon the sin of others, but upon their suffering. For him, sin was, above all, the refusal of compassion for the suffering of others, the refusal to think beyond the horizon of one's own history of suffering. Sin was for him what Augustine later called the "heart's curving back on itself," the abandoning of oneself to the secret narcissism of the creature. Thus, Christianity began as a community of memory and narrative committed to the discipleship of Jesus whose first glance embraced the suffering of others.

There are parables of Jesus in which through their telling he entered the memory of humanity in a special way. One of them is the parable of the "Good Samaritan," which he relates as an answer to the question: "Who is my neighbor?" In our context, the question is: For whom am I responsible? To whom am I accountable? One insight emerges crystal clear from this parable told in the images of a provincial society of ancient times: this realm of responsibility, this area of accountability, cannot be unambiguously outlined and defined by us in advance.

The "neighbor" and thereby the partner to our responsibility is never only the person whom we imagine and accept as such. The range of our responsibility is in principle unlimited. The criterion for its measure and extent is—and remains—the suffering of the other, just like the man in Jesus' parable, who fell among thieves and whom the priest and the Levite pass by for the sake of a "worthier cause." Whoever is looking for "God," in the sense that Jesus describes, does not know of any "worthier cause" that would excuse him or her. A person who speaks of "God," in the sense that Jesus does, accepts the risk that the misfortune of outsiders may damage his or her own preconceived certainties. Thus, to talk about this God means that one simply must find expression for the suffering of the stranger. A theology learned in Jesus' school about God is one full of empathy.

The taking of suffering into memory becomes thereby the basis of a universal responsibility by always taking into account the suffering of the others, the suffering of the foreigner and—what is genuinely biblical—even the suffering of the enemy. And this other's suffering is then not forgotten when one considers one's own history of suffering. (I always had the suspicion that when Jesus was talking about loving one's neighbor, he was thinking primarily of the love of one's enemies.) This memory of the other's suffering is not only the moral basis for the synchronic understanding between human beings; it reaches deep into the diachronic political landscape of our world. For this there are examples, examples of a "war of memories" as well as examples for a "peace of memories."

In the former Yugoslavia, the memories of suffering became the burial shroud for a whole nation and the gallows for any attempt at understanding between ethnic groups. Here the individual peoples remembered only their own histories of suffering, and thus this purely self-referential *memoria passionis* did not grow into a source of dialogue and peace, but became a source of enmity, of hate, and of violence. The fact that Christian denominations also participated in this staged production of memories of suffering makes the process worse and more painful. We can but hope that the present situation between Israel and Palestine will be different. One scene remains for me unforgettable: when the Israeli Izaak Rabin and the Palestinian Yassar Arafat took each other's hand and mutually pledged that they would not only consider their own suffering, but that they were ready to remember and take into account also the suffering of the others, the suffering of the former enemies. This is essentially politics of peace from a biblical *memoria passionis*! I know that the movement toward understanding on this basis is extremely fragile, that it has already cost great sacrifices and will cost more. But is there an alternative? And is there one for Ireland?

The Authority of the Suffering

In the present debates about a "global *ethos*" or a "world culture," there is often mentioned an ethical universalism which is to grow on the basis of a minimal consensus laboriously added together, or perhaps simply cleverly concocted. Yet this ethical universalism can develop, if at all, only on the basis of a fundamental consensus between peoples and cultures that has to be continually regained and that is constantly being threatened. There is, indeed, one authority that is recognized in all great cultures and religions and that has not been superseded by any critique of authority: the authority of those who are suffering.

This authority cannot first be prepared for hermeneutically, nor can it be secured through discursive argument. With regard to this authority, obedience comes before understanding—and, indeed, unconditionally, at the price of being moral at all. This authority does not have to be further justified; toward it, there is for moral reasoning no possibility of a refusal to obey its command, perhaps by invoking the concept of "autonomy." In this sense the encounter with the suffering of the other is a kind of "state of emergency," something not based on general rules which one could then use to hide behind. For me, as a Christian theologian, this authority is the only authority in which the authority of the judging God is manifested in the world for all peoples. Through obedience to it, moral conscience is formed; what we call the voice of conscience is our reaction to accepting the presence among us of this alien suffering. It is well-known that Jesus, in his parable of the Last Judgment in Matthew 25 (again, one of those stories with which he entered into people's hearts), submitted the entire history of humanity to this criterion: "Whatever you did to the least of my brothers and sisters you did to me . . . whatever you failed to do for one of the least of these, you failed to do for me."

To respect alien suffering is the condition of all great culture (even if there is no culture, as Walter Benjamin rightly supposed, that does not contain within it a certain element of barbarism). And the bringing of the suffering of others to expression is the presupposition of all universalist claims, including and especially those of Christianity. Thus it could be that the "weak" category of *memoria passionis* succeeds in going beyond the kind of Christian thinking in terms of identity in which only the circular self-understanding of a specific culture, namely the Western-European civilization, is mirrored and reaffirmed. This Western culture, despite its universalistic orientation, has always found it difficult, and still finds it so today, to perceive adequately the worlds of experience and discourse of other cultures. The "weak" taking into memory of alien suffering, and the narratives formed by this memory, could prove a powerful force enabling communication between religions and cultures, and with this become aware of the great number of the histories of suffering in the world—for example, in the encounter with the ethics of compassion of the great Asian religions, especially of Buddhism (which is, granted, quite diverse in itself). In recognizing the authority of those suffering, the monotheistic religions could, I think, find a meeting point with Eastern religions and cultures.

It is true that the biblical traditions do not speak primarily about a morality, but about a hope. Their speaking about God does not culminate in an ethics, but in an eschatology. Yet it is precisely in this orientation, despite the supposed or the actual powerlessness and lack of vision, that one finds the strength not simply to abandon or arbitrarily to minimize the standards of responsibility. I know that it is difficult to rescue this kind of universal responsibility from the suspicion of overblown abstraction. And without continually refocusing the priorities of our commitment, one cannot move ahead. Yet, it is precisely the desperate situation of the choices that we face that confirms the premise that our scope of responsibility is not shrinking and being reduced to smaller, more local situations, as is often suggested by a postmodern outlook, but rather, that it is continuing to expand. The promise, for instance, that Europe will be a blossoming rather than a burning multicultural landscape, a landscape of peace and not a landscape of imploding violence and escalating civil wars, also has its moral price. The payment has yet to be made.

An Era of Cultural Amnesia?

Friedrich Nietzsche tried to write the epitaph for Christianity: "All the possibilities of Christian life, the most intense and the most relaxed, the most harmless and thoughtless, and the most reflected upon have been thoroughly tried; it is time to invent something new . . ." And he linked his "new way of living" to the triumph of cultural amnesia, which increasingly molds our "post-modern" landscape and in which tradition-orientated religions and worldviews are ever more threatened with disappearance. "Yet in the smallest and in the greatest happiness there is always one thing that makes happiness be happiness. . . . Whoever is not able to sit down on the threshold of the moment, forgetting all the pasts, whoever cannot stand on one spot like a goddess of victory without dizziness and fear, will never know what happiness is. . . ."[2] The archetype of happiness would thus be the amnesia of the victor; its precondition, the merciless forgetting of the victims. This is indeed totally contrary to the biblical mindset of covenant and the anamnestic solidarity demanded by this covenant. It is completely opposed to the significance of *memoria,* especially of the *memoria passionis* which is woven into the Christian understanding of peace and happiness. The vision of the God of biblical traditions stands opposed to the attempt to fix the happiness of the human family at the price of its amnesia.

The contemporary triumph of amnesia supports itself on various pillars. One of them, in my opinion, is theology itself. In constructing its notion of history, has it not always used much too "strong" categories which gloss over far too quickly all the violent interruptions in history, all the gaping wounds, all the disasters and catastrophes. And then, has it not "protected" its talk about God from the pain of memory? Should not at least a catastrophe such as that of Auschwitz operate as an ultimatum against an all-too pliable theological treatment of history? At least now, should not the question arise about the standing and the significance of this horror in the midst of the *Logos* of theology? Should not, at the very least, theology now be convinced that it cannot itself heal all wounds? That it is simply no longer possible for it to conceptualize the identity of Christianity—once again, similar to Plato's ideas or in a fashionable turn from history to psychology—only as a gnostic myth of redemption divorced from history?

2. Nietzsche, *Use and Abuse of History,* 6.

To be sure, even modern science and scholarship do not simply break the spell of the cultural amnesia here referred to. In our civilization, science is the essence of normality, and in this sense it can be said of it, too, that it heals all wounds and does not know the pain of remembering. Especially with regard to the academic discipline of history, I would like to make a comment: if I am right, since the so-called German *Historikerstreif* (the controversy among historians on whether the atrocities committed under the reign of National Socialism are just one more instance of the violation of human rights, or whether this program of mass annihilation of the European Jews needs to be evaluated as unique and outstanding in the history of humankind), the standpoint of "historicizing" National Socialism and its crimes has more or less won the day. Certainly, this catastrophe cannot simply be taken out of history, it cannot be allowed to be stylized into a kind of negative myth, into a tragedy beyond history. To do this would then simply amount to losing the standpoint of responsibility, of shame and radical change. Yet, in view of Auschwitz, for me the question remains how a horror that threatens—again and again—to evade being historically conceived, can nonetheless be kept in memory. This can succeed only with a way of writing history which is itself supported by an anamnestic culture, a culture of remembering, a historiography which is also aware of the kind of forgetting that reigns in every historicizing objectification.

"*Wissenschaft* heals all wounds": Is not this belief also true for large and prominent sections of contemporary philosophy? "Israel or Athens: Where does Anamnestic Reason Belong?": this is the title of a text with which the German social philosopher Jürgen Habermas tried to prove to me that the anamnestic spirit of the biblical concept of time has long since been taken up by the concept of reasoning in European philosophy.[3] In this way, it would seem that at least with the defenses of professional European philosophy, the dangers of cultural amnesia can be resisted. But then why does, for example, the catastrophe of Auschwitz appear in Habermas's work only in his *Small Political Writings*—and there,

3. Habermas, *Liberating Power of Symbols*, 78–89.

as is well known, it does appear in a both decisive and influential way—but not, not even with one word, in his great philosophical writings on communicative reason? Does not communicative theory also heal all wounds? But how is it possible then to speak in a generalizable way of what remains as evil (*Unheil*), of what cannot be healed, of what should not be allowed to disappear behind the shield of cultural amnesia, of what cannot be contained within seamless normality? How can one speak of something that, if at all, needs another kind of forgiving than the forgiving that time produces when it is said to heal all wounds, or the forgiveness imparted by a theory which covers them over?

What remains when it appears that all wounds have been closed is difficult to describe. There is a peculiar sense of something missing, a sense that resists having the pain of remembering being totally alleviated, be it in a "purely theoretical" way, be it in a psychological or aesthetical way, be it in a commemorative service or even in a "religious" way. In the present age, this experience of missing something can hardly be understood if one, as usually happens, turns it into a typical condition of the older generation. Yet even more, this experience of something missing manifests itself with the younger generation; it nourishes the skepticism of the young, their indifference, sometimes also their anger with regard to what the older generations have to offer them as *the* experience, *the* view of things, *the* lesson from history which is then elevated to the canon of normality. What strikes me in the contemporary discussion about Daniel Goldhagen and his book about "the ordinary Germans and the Holocaust" is that the almost unanimous criticism of the experts (which according to the criteria of professional historiography seems justified) was not able to put to rest the worries of many, especially young people, about the extent of this history of guilt.

The *memoria passionis* as remembering alien suffering remains a fragile category in a time in which people believe they can finally protect themselves only with the weapon of forgetting, with the shield of amnesia against the histories of suffering and evil deeds which continue to pour in: yesterday, Auschwitz; today, Bosnia and Rwanda; and tomorrow . . . ? But even this forgetting is not without consequences. Something that has always deeply affected and disturbed me in the situation "after Auschwitz" was the unhappiness and the desperation of those who survived this catastrophe. So much unspeakable unhappiness, so many suicides! Here, clearly, human beings have collapsed under the despair about what human beings are "capable" of doing to other human beings. Thus Auschwitz has greatly lowered among human beings the metaphysical and moral boundary below which one still feels shame. Only the forgetful have overlooked something like this. Or those who supposedly have been successful in forgetting that there is something they have forgotten. But they do not remain untouched. The wound has not closed. One cannot, not even in the name of humanity, sin whenever and wherever. Not only the individual human person, but also the "idea" of the human person and of humanity, is vulnerable; indeed, it can be destroyed. Only a few connect the present crises of humanity, the so-called "decline in values"—the increasing degree of deafness against "great" claims, the crisis of solidarity, an extreme modesty about one's own ability (a modesty cleverly adapted to each situation), and so forth—few connect these traits of contemporary culture with the crisis that Auschwitz signifies as well as with the more recent catastrophes which also have fallen victim to cultural amnesia.

There is not only a superficial history of the human species, there is also a deeper history, and it is indeed vulnerable. Do not the orgies of rape and violence in our time acquire something like the normative power of the factual? Do they not—behind the shield of amnesia—corrode the "basic trust of civilization," those moral and cultural reserves in which the humanity of human beings is rooted? How much of these resources are still available? How far have they already been exhausted? Does what is happening here amount to bidding farewell to a concept of the human person as it has been familiar to us in history? Could it be that not only has God become lost to men and women under the spell of this cultural amnesia, but that the human person herself is going missing more and more, by losing what up to now has been called emphatically her "humanity"? What remains after we have once again successfully closed all the wounds? When cultural amnesia has been completed? The human person? Which human person? Man as computerized intelligence who is not able to remember anything because—just like a computerized robot—he is also not able to forget anything, thus, an intelligence without history, without the ability to suffer and without morality?

In his book *The Clash of Civilizations?* the American writer Samuel Huntington envisages that the global conflicts of tomorrow will not only be defined by political blocks of power, but by the conflict of civilizations or cultures. For many, his thesis is controversial; the question contained within it, however, remains explosive. The conflict of Western culture with other cultures, for example, and especially with the culture of Islam, can indeed be described as the conflict between one cultural world that is guided by remembrance and another "modern" world that is to a great degree guided by discourse. It becomes evident that cultures guided by remembrance have distinctive disadvantages against those led by discourse. They contain obstacles to modernity of a special kind; they paralyze curiosity, are suspicious of experiments, ritualize their lifeworld, and are too much orientated toward mere repetition; they become trapped in fundamentalisms all too easily.

But what type of cultures would there be without any kind of a uniting, binding memory, cultures which then are exclusively discourse-oriented, cultures whose memory is ruled by discourse, but whose memory cannot guide discourse? Will human beings in them end up being anything more than an unlimited experiment upon themselves, humans who are threatened more and more with going under in the technological whirlpools that they have set in motion? How will the European West, if it is based on a cultural amnesia, be able to weather the oncoming challenges and conflicts? The future of European modernity, as well as the recognition of the dignity of other cultural worlds, rests upon the rescue of a cultural memory, itself guided by the taking into memory of the suffering of others.

Translated by Peter P. Kenny

CHAPTER 6

Memoria Passionis

A Fundamental Category of Political Theology[1]

Two Political Theologies

THE CONCEPT OF POLITICAL theology goes back to pre-Christian traditions. We encounter it today mostly in two forms: one within the framework of governmental and legal theories and the other in a more strictly theological context. They differ from each other in their evaluation of European modernity and their corollary understandings of "political."

The use of political theology in political and legal philosophy will only be mentioned in a brief historical overview. It grows out of the intentions of "political theology" in the past. In the end, talking about political theology goes back to the Stoa and its three-part division of mythical, natural, and political.[2] In ancient Rome, this political theology actually served as religious legitimation of absolute and infallible states. Reflections of this Roman political state metaphysics can be found in early Christian theologies, for example, in the Byzantine state theology of Eusebius. After the Renaissance, this Roman political theology was again reinterpreted by Machiavelli and then by Hobbes. Finally, Roman political theology had an effect on the Enlightenment and the democratic critique

---

1. Metz, *Memoria Passionis*, 252–57.

2. For a description and critique of this division by Varro, see Augustine, *De Civitate Dei*, VI:5.

of French Traditionalism as well as on the Restorationist idea of a Christian state as held by political Romantics, as we see in the political philosophy of the Hegelian Right. In the atmosphere of these traditions, Carl Schmitt was able in the last century to put forward his "political theology" (first in 1922) and to ground his opposition to the Weimar Republic and to parliamentary democracy in a decisionist concept of the state. Schmitt's political theology, which has gained new attention in our times of increasing uncertainty, is only theological—if it is theological at all—in the sense that it understands all legal concepts of government as secularized theological concepts. The relationship of the political theology of Carl Schmitt to the thought of Leo Strauss, which is often seen to be important for understanding the current administration in Washington and the recent history of the reception of Schmitt in Europe and the USA, cannot be discussed here.[3]

Distinct from this is the strong theological use of the concept of political theology. It is grounded in a theology of the world, in a theology done "facing the world." It is concerned with a theological assessment of the processes of the modern Enlightenment—in particular with the differentiation of state and society and the concomitant expansion of the concept "political"—but without a blind and undialectical adherence to the internal contradictions of the Enlightenment. Sometime in the mid-sixties, I introduced that concept into the theological discussion and tried to develop it as an approach to fundamental theology under the name of "the new political theology."[4] In order to emphasize the theological character of this new political theology within the above mentioned threefold classical structure of theology (mythical, natural,

3. For more about this as well as a sense of the relationship of this classical political theology to the concept of the new political theology, see Manemann, *Carl Schmitt*.

4. See my *Zum Begriff der neuen Politischen Theologie*, as well as my forward to the fifth edition of *Glaube in Geschichte und Gesellschaft*. The strictly theological character of the new political theology becomes clear in the theological biography by Peters, *Johann Baptist Metz*. See also Ashley, *Interruptions*, as well as Reikerstorfer, "Im 'Theodizeeblick,'" 105–27.

political), political theology should really be counted as natural, which is to say, philosophical theology.

The first concern of this new political theology was snatching Christian talk about God back from the private sphere. This privatization, a "modern" reaction to the Enlightenment, had produced the separation of religion and society apparent in post-scholastic (existential, personal, and transcendental) Catholic theology. This new political theology also wanted to reformulate the eschatological message of Christianity within the changed structural conditions of the public sphere. It defined the church as an institution of the social and critical freedom of faith and characterized its Christian spirituality as a unity of the mystical and political—a mysticism of open eyes. This new political theology confirmed the biblical roots of its God-talk by referring to the tradition of Job, to the "negative theology" of the prophets, to apocalyptic wisdom, and to the motifs of the kingdom of God and discipleship. Although it criticized the above-mentioned tendency to privatization in modern theology, even in the "anthropocentric turn" of Karl Rahner, it remained faithful to some his central themes.[5] From the start, this type of political theology gained ecumenical relevance. So, for example, J. Moltmann connected his *Theology of Hope* (1964) with these same intentions, and D. Sölle formulated her critique of Bultmann's existentialist hermeneutic as *Political Theology* (1971). The influence of D. Bonhoeffer's and of S. Kierkegaard's critical interpretation of church and society are obviously a part of this theology's ecumenical background. Also important in this connection would be the Jewish perspective in J. Taubes' *Eschatology* (1947) and especially in his *The Theology of Paul* (1987), as well as the beginning of a new interpretation of the two-kingdoms doctrine.

5. See Peters, "Karl Rahner und die neue Politische Theologie," 43–50; see also Martinez, *Confronting the Mystery of God*, 21–88.

The New Political Theology as a Fundamental Theology
ex Memoria Passionis

As a fundamental theology, this new political theology tries to take into account the fact that metaphysical questions have lost their social, historical, and cultural innocence. "Who is speaking of God—when, where, for whom, and with what intent?" Such questions are constitutive of theological questioning—which now has to discuss subjectivity, *praxis*, and otherness.[6] This questioning was the main way in which the new political theology initially influenced liberation theology.

Accordingly, the new political theology understands, for example, the catastrophe of Auschwitz as belonging to the internal structure of Christian talk about God and so refuses to retreat into a mechanistic (subjectless) historical idealism. It is for this reason considered a post-idealist theology with a special sensitivity for theodicy. It turns itself against any talk about God which attempts to find the final reasons for suffering, for it suspects such explanations would ban eschatological questions to God in the face of the public history of suffering in his creation. Consequently, this fundamental theology seeks to find universalism and the possibility of truth by using the category of *memoria passionis*, the "remembrancing" of others' suffering. For this theology, only in that history which is a history of human suffering is there a truthful Grand Narrative. For this reason, it criticizes a modern idea of reason which tries to evade the dialectical tension between remembering and forgetting and thus maintains the cultural amnesia of our modern or postmodern societies. Very early on, the new political theology stressed the anamnestic basis for theology's *logos*, for its talk about God and his Christ—by referring to "dangerous memories,"[7] and it dealt with the theme of history using the idea of "the future in the memory of suffering."[8]

6. Only in this way can one discern the theological meaning of the self, existence, and individualization, in short, the meaning of faithful existence.

7. See my "'Politische Theologie' in der Diskussion," 267–301.

8. See, for example, my article, "Zukunft aus dem Gedächtnis des Leidens," 399–407.

Finally, a central theological challenge for the new political theology becomes finding a way into the socially fragmented and culturally polycentric world church of the post-Vatican II era. A social reality which directly contradicts the gospel with its degradation, exploitation, and racism demands from theology a way of speaking about God in terms of contradiction and change as a "dangerous memory." This change certainly must include the possibility of guilt and the necessity for reflection on concrete historical subjects: this should remove the basis for hate and violence in political change.

And in today's profound pluralism of religious and cultural worlds, the new political theology is focused on a hermeneutic of acknowledgment, one which avoids cultural relativism by making the authority of those who suffer axiomatic for all cultural and religious dialogues as well as for any "politics of acknowledgement." As a fundamental theology, this new political theology wants to bring validity to the ongoing claim of biblical talk about God in pluralistic societies. A monotheism sensitive to suffering and a Christology sensitive to theodicy confront an oblivious public realm with the humanizing power of *memoria passionis*.

Christianity in a Truly Pluralistic Public Sphere

The new political theology has tried from the beginning—in an early program of deprivatization—to break free from that self-privatizing theology which was a reaction to the spirit of European modernity. In the face of the dramatically increasing pluralism of religions and cultures in globalization, in the face of a truly pluralistic public sphere, there is a new danger of Christianity privatizing itself. I have dealt with the danger of self-privatization by proposing a church of compassion and by suggesting a European public realm with a *de facto* freedom of religion. I have also formulated the basic claim of Christianity to remember God as a provocative *memoria passionis* in the completely pluralist common public realm of our society. Political theology as a theology is nothing but an attempt to talk about God while facing the contemporary world.

Translated by John K. Downey

CHAPTER 7

The Elephant with Hope

Katholische Nachrichten-Agentur, KNA:[1] Professor Metz, how do you see the church today?

JBM: It's really not the time for a new Council, and it's not the time for a groundbreaking synod like the one twenty-five years ago. This is a time-out from great events. The misunderstandings on one side and the disappointments on the other are piling up. Crises, it seems, are becoming permanent. It's no longer about paths out of the crisis, but rather paths within the crisis.

KNA: What would these paths look like?

JBM: I don't know of a good answer. I do have, however, an image, a metaphor I've known for some time: it is the metaphor of the elephant, the Catholic elephant which has already lumbered across the thresholds of many epochs—although somewhat laboriously. Let me clarify this metaphor a bit for our situation. The Catholic Church, with a billion Catholics around the world, is still as big and massive as an elephant. It is endowed with an elephant's memory in which world history and intellectual history, cultural history,

1. Interview conducted by Michael Jackqueman (Metz, "Elephant with Hope," 1–2). My thanks to Benjamin Downey for sharing his translation of the Italian version of the interview. Metz was the author of the German Bishop's Statement, *Our Hope* (1975), in which the synod sought to implement Vatican Council II.

and religious history are preserved as in no other place: the liberating and the burdensome, the illuminating and the obscuring. The Catholic Church remains thick-skinned and stubborn like an elephant in two respects: first, it is thick-skinned when it comes to the allure and seduction of the *Zeitgeist*, of the spirit of the times; its thick skin serves as a productive non-contemporaneity. Second, the Church remains even more thick-skinned when it comes to those who sit on high and dictate the route for the elephant.

KNA: Which paths should the elephant follow?

JBM: Actually, many things are changing in the Catholic Church, but in a rather amorphous, you might say, passive way, under the anonymous pressure of unknown, indefinite conditions. It needs a well thought out change, authentic reform. Otherwise a danger looms for the Christianity of the Church, a danger which may sound undramatic, but which in my view is an elemental force. Namely, the Church may harden into a bourgeois service church, a stabilization of that service church which in our dream of the church we imagined was already behind us. The number of people leaving the church will presumably continue to decrease, but indifference within the church will grow even more. In a diffuse and confusing world, the need for frameworks for living increases immeasurably. As a framework for living, the church will therefore continue to be respected in this world. But what are her chances as a representative of a way of life? Permit me to once again use the metaphor of the elephant, to inquire into the proverbial sensibility of this great beast and ask whether the "sensitive soul" of the Catholic elephant could provide a sense of direction.

KNA: What would be the compass for this orientation?

JBM: This sensitive soul of the elephant would, in my view, be a church of compassion, a church of engaged awareness of others' suffering, a church whose compassion expresses its passion for God. For the biblical message of God is, at its core, a message sensitive to suffering, sensitive to the suffering of others, even to the suffering of enemies. I have stressed this so much because from the beginning, the church, like Christianity, had great difficulty with this fundamental sensitivity to suffering in the biblical message. The question of justice for innocent victims, which troubles the biblical traditions, was very early and very quickly—too quickly—transformed and turned into a question of the salvation of the guilty party. The Christian doctrine of salvation dramatized too much the question of guilt and relativized too much the question of suffering. Christianity transformed itself from a religion primarily sensitive to suffering into a religion primarily sensitive to guilt. The church, it seems, has always found it easier to deal with the guilty perpetrators than with the innocent victims.

KNA: Will Christians today even understand what you mean by the word "compassion"?

JBM: First, I must confess that I do not know any suitable German word for what I mean by the engaged awareness of the suffering of others. *Mitleid* (pity) sounds too non-political and is suspected of papering over unjust and innocent suffering with sentimentality. So I have decided on the English word "compassion." It may well be that many consider this Christianity of compassion to be a vague pastoral romanticism. Certainly, this compassion is a great provocation, just like Christianity in general, just like discipleship, just like God. But Jesus did not look first to the sin of others, but rather to the suffering of others. It's hard to explain this in the language of a rigid bourgeois religion, a religion which fears nothing more than its own failure and so always prefers the bird in its hand to the two in the bush. We must instead rely on traces of an enduring sympathy, on an unflinching willingness not to avoid the suffering of others; we must commit to alliances and grassroots projects of compassion that elude the present current of refined indifference and cultivated apathy, and that refuse to live and celebrate happiness and love exclusively as narcissistic self-dramatization. Finally, let me return briefly to the image of the Catholic elephant, to these billions of Catholics. If, in their various walks of life, they risked proceeding with this experiment of compassion and if, in the end, they arrived at an ecumenism of compassion among all Christians, would this not throw a new light on our globalized and, at the same time, so painfully divided world?

Translated by John K. Downey

Part III

Mystical and Political

CHAPTER 8

Under the Spell of Cultural Amnesia?

An Example from Europe and Its Consequences

I.

EUROPE, THE EUROPE OF the EU, is having trouble with itself these days. Which "Europe" is intended, and what kind of Europe is wanted? In the discussions about adopting the EU-Constitution (or more precisely, the contract for an EU-Constitution) in the past few years, one could hear over and again: "Europe is a secular project—Christianity therefore has no place in a European constitution." We need to pay closer attention here—especially with regard to the meaning of "secular," as well as with regard to the religious neutrality of the constitution that follows from "Europe as a secular project." There are two directly opposed versions of this neutrality. One may be designated the secularistic (*laizistische*) version, the other the pluralistic version; correspondingly, the spiritual-moral climate of the new Europe would be characterized as either a-religious or religiously plural.

The pluralistic version of the constitutional contract would not ban religion from the public sphere, but would locate its value in a constitutional pluralism of worldviews and religions. It would do this by constitutionally guaranteeing religious freedom, a religious freedom that would be positive as well as negative, providing protection "for" religion as well as protection "from" religion.

Against this, the a-religious version (something that can really be understood only in a historically French constellation) comes down to a strict privatization of religion. This version is not really neutral regarding religion, because its concept of neutrality inevitably privileges negative religious freedom (freedom from religion). It is anti-pluralist to the core. The secularistic *ethos* of a European constitution would overwhelm in a fundamentalist manner all those national constitutions in Europe which deal with religion in public life in a different way (than in France).[1]

It might well be that these days there is more than a little to be suspicious about in this "secular" version of the developing European constitutional *ethos*. I myself can recognize in it only a kind of "patina-vision" for Europe, a vision that ignores the growing insight today into how the dialectical processes of a one-dimensional Enlightenment and a leveling secularization are full of contradictions. The a-religious version seeks to subject the developing European public sphere (quasi-fundamentalistically) to an undialectical secularization paradigm.

In this connection, I would like to at least briefly mention a current discussion in philosophy of religion in Germany. I have always wondered why the Frankfurt School has never really moved beyond its early "dialectic of Enlightenment" to speak of a "dialectic of secularization." For example, it seems to me that the later work of Jürgen Habermas opens up the possibility of a new philosophical "translation" of the substance of religion. In this "translation," philosophy (of religion) doesn't simply replace the authentic language of religion in order to make religion superfluous to the public discourse of modernity and to its normative integration of constitutional pluralism.[2] As Habermas says,

> The guarantee of equal ethical freedoms demands the
> secularization of state authority, but it forbids the political overextension of the secular worldview. Secularized
> citizens, insofar as they remain in their roles as citizens,

1. See Weiler, *Ein christliches Europa*, and the forword by Böckenförde that also contains important and stimulating ideas regarding the difference between a secular and a pluralistic Europe. On the whole first part of my reflections, see also Casanova, "Der Ort der Religion."

2. See Reikerstorfer, "Jüdisch-christliches Erbe," 30–34.

may neither fundamentally deny the potential for truth
in religious worldviews nor restrict the right of their
believing fellow citizens to make contributions to public
discussions using religious language. A liberal political
culture might even expect its secularized members to
make efforts to translate relevant contributions from religious language into publicly accessible speech.[3]

Critical questions admittedly also appear over against this quasi-
operational definition of a "dialectic of secularization" within
the framework of a liberal discourse community. Doesn't the
discourse-theoretical approach of Habermas undervalue the
intelligible and critical power of the anamnestic basis for public
discourse, a power that, through the Jewish-Christian tradition,
has penetrated not only the *ethos* of faith but the *ethos* of human
rationality, as well? And wasn't this reflected, for example, within
the Frankfurt School itself in the negative metaphysics of Walter
Benjamin and Theodor W. Adorno?[4]

II.

Indeed, I have never missed the anamnestic basis of public discourse more than in the discussions of the contract for the EU-
Constitution. Understandably such an appeal to this anamnestic
base would have to be justified in terms of whether and how a
remembrance-oriented public sphere—especially in the face of
European history—actually can be the foundation for understanding and peace. Wouldn't this instead radically damage or even
revoke one of the most important achievements of the political
Enlightenment? Isn't it precisely historically and culturally rooted
collective memories that always hinder mutual understanding,
that continually have led to painful conflicts and dramatic quar-
rels (between and within nations) and therefore have nourished all

3. Habermas, *Zwischen Naturalismus und Religion*, 322. Habermas speaks
expressly in this connection of the "path to a dialectical understanding of cultural secularization."

4. In addition see Metz, "Vernunft mit Leidensapriori," 25–31.

open or latent civil wars into the present day? I have tried to meet this danger by formulating *memoria passionis* as a basic category for doing theology in a pluralistic public sphere. This offers a way of dealing with the pluralistic public sphere that is accessible and reasonable to all men and women without retreating to a formal, purely procedural discourse rationality.[5]

With regard to the discussion of the EU constitutional contract that has been going on in the meantime, it appears as if Europe has lost its memory. It's as if this memory has been sacrificed to that progressive cultural amnesia that evidently many Europeans take for real progress.[6]

The preamble of the EU constitutional contract is concerned with the spiritual and moral climate of Europe, in short, the European *ethos*. This *ethos* is described there exclusively in terms of universal attributes like "cultural, religious, humanistic" which are divorced from history. But there is no way to determine the European *ethos* without historical remembrancing, without identifying and securing the historical-cultural deep structures of Europe! Yes, democracy is rooted in consensus, but the democratic *ethos* is rooted in remembrance. This remembrance makes it possible to account for how the "heritages" (culture, religion, humanism) cited abstractly in the EU Constitution did not develop in isolation but interpenetrate each other, shaping the European *ethos* in a crisscrossing of mutual criticism and inspiration.

5. See my new book, *Memoria Passionis*.

6. At the end of this "progress" stands the biotechnological "human experiment" that no longer allows itself to be constrained by normative appeals to remembrance. In the public dispute over the "human image" and "values," Christianity emphasizes that human beings are not only subjects of their own experimentation, but more fundamentally subjects of their own memory. Christianity does this in support of a politics of memory which objects to the looming total self-reproduction of the human being in biotechnological experiment. For this (anamnestic) politics, the human person is and remains more and other than the last, not yet fully experimentally fixed bit of nature. Finally, in this public dispute the currently prevailing discourse politics can only prevent itself from being overpowered by an ever-expanding bio-politics through relying on a memory-sharpened semantic addressing the theme "human being."

Finally, it is no accident that the secular state (the state whose secularity derives from its guarantee of religious freedom and protection of neutrality) arose in a particular historical-cultural sphere shaped by the Jewish-Christian heritage.

In this sense, the practical religious freedom that arose in secular Europe also has biblical roots. They lead finally not to a non-religious Europe but to a religiously plural Europe. These biblical roots show through, for example, in the understanding of the Reformation churches as "religions of freedom" and on the Catholic side the lately (too late?) declared readiness to unconditionally respect the "the sanctity of conscience" in public religious discourse. This formulation, partly derived from a papal encyclical, is affirmed by the small but momentous "Decree on Religious Freedom" of the Second Vatican Council in which the Catholic Church orders and subordinates the abstract right of the truth to the right of the person in truth. Shouldn't this biblical heritage be expressly named in the preamble to a European constitution—and precisely in the interest of normatively securing full practical religious freedom and the pluralism rooted therein?

III.

I would like to add two comments. One refers to the situation of the church in a Europe threatened by the spell of cultural amnesia. The other concerns the meaning of *memoria passionis* as a provocative remembrance in the struggle for the future of humanity in an age of cultural amnesia.

First

The "dialectic of secularization" suggested above leads in any case not to a public sphere free of religion but to a public sphere characterized by pluralism of religions and worldviews. In this situation, it seems to me a new and elementary danger for Christianity is emerging: it is not so much (or at least not primarily)

the danger of the secular state extrinsically imposing a privatization of Christian faith; it is much more the danger that Christians under the anonymous pressure of a religiously pluralistic
public sphere increasingly will privatize Christianity themselves
and thereby call into question their identity and mission. European Christianity is threatened not just by the danger of self-
secularization but more precisely the danger of itself privatizing
whatever cannot be secularized.

This is why for several years I have been trying to develop
a deprivatization program under the heading of a new "political
theology."[7] This political theology should break open any self-
privatization by modern theology in reaction to the challenges of
modernity, particularly the challenges of the Enlightenment and
secularization. It also addresses a second phase of deprivatization
by overcoming the tendency of the Christian church to privatize
itself.

Is our European world, a world in which the project of modernity has succeeded, a strictly post-traditional society? Admittedly,
one cannot revitalize dead or withered traditions by showing how
necessary they really would be or all that they might achieve—for
instance in the face of that collective angst and uncertainty which
often times overlay and paralyze public discourse today. The real
issue is different and goes something like this: Are there at the
margins of modernity, in the transition to the postmodern, still
institutions which understand themselves as accumulated memories, as the public encodings of a long-term cultural remembrance,
as providers of a storehouse of memory for structuring diffuse life-
worlds that cannot be mastered purely discursively? Are there still
institutions that can effectively get control over what has become a
reflexive engagement with traditions and bring the indispensabil-
ity of traditions from aporetic formulation to political and cultural

7. The new political theology should not be confused with those former
"political theologies" like the "classical" threefold division of theology—
mythical, natural, political theology—familiar since the Stoics. If this new
political theology must be assigned a place in this threefold division, it would
belong to "natural" (that is, philosophical) theology. See Metz, "Politische
Theologie," 392–94.

validity? Are there still institutions which can serve as carriers and mediators of a pre-linguistic point of reference? Are there still such institutions, and if there are, don't religious institutions especially belong among them? And doesn't the "elephant's memory" of the church also belong there?

Admittedly, such a definition of classical religious institutions can only with difficulty evade the suspicion that it is a negligent idealization. It is—in the perspective of the Christian religion—only through witnessing that the religious institution, the church, brings together publicly in herself that which her remembrance of faith compels her to: the indivisible unity of love of God and love of neighbor, of God's suffering and suffering with others, of a passion for God and compassion, of remembering God in remembrancing the suffering of others. The church as an institution must in its (liturgical) representation of the authority of God always also represent, embody, and proclaim its own subordination to the undeniable authority of those who suffer.

Second

Does there not exist a danger that a Europe which openly admits its biblical roots will increasingly find itself trapped in the global struggles of religion and culture? The first thing to ask is this: What is it that could prevent our globalized world from imploding into uncontrollable religious and cultural strife (here Christianity, there Islam, here the West, there the Arab world)? What is it that can bring our world together peacefully during these times of globalization? I will attempt an extremely brief reply.

The proposition of a fundamental equality among all human beings—the deepest and still most unsatisfied assumption about humanity—has a biblical basis. The moral implication, adopted by Christianity and proclaimed in its message of the indivisible unity of the love of God and the love of neighbor, of God's suffering and suffering with others, is this: there is no suffering in the world that does not concern us. This proposition refers to the recognition of an authority that is reasonable and accessible to all human beings: the authority of those who suffer, of unjust and innocent suffering. It is an authority which obliges all human beings before any consensus and agreement and which therefore neither culture and religion nor the church can subvert or relativize. For this reason, the recognition of this authority would be that criterion which is able to orient religious and cultural discourse in a globalized world. It would ground an *ethos* of peace for a pluralistic and globalized public sphere. And a European politics that acknowledges this biblical legacy with its demand for compassion (as well as the Greek legacy of theoretical inquiry and Roman antiquity's legacy of republican legal thinking about rights and the state) would be more and other than the mere executor of the market and technology and their so-called practical constraints in these times of globalization.

Translated by John K. Downey and Steven Ostovich

CHAPTER 9

This Pope Is Good for a Few Surprises

Süddeutsche Zeitung:[1] *One of the first reactions to the election of Joseph Ratzinger is often questioning whether the Holy Spirit was in attendance at the papal conclave. What's your opinion?*

JBM: If the Spirit has ever been present, he was certainly present this time. The Holy Spirit is a sort of divine version of surprise and no one disputes that this election was a surprise.

SZ: What does that tell us?

JBM: The late pope opened up a new global stage for the Church's "Catholicity," chiefly through striking gestures and symbols. In this way, John Paul II led his Church into a new anteroom of ecumenism—especially in respect to the religion of "the elder brothers," the Jews—and encouraged the Church to engage with other cultures. Admittedly these symbolic maneuvers can only become *functional* if they are updated theologically, theologically informed. I have to and I want to have confidence that Benedict XVI has the theological authority to accomplish this task.

Ratzinger now acts more or less as the final authority, no longer as an advisor. This new role will confront him with the challenge of

1. Interview conducted by Alexander Kissler (Metz, *Gespräche, Interviews, Antworten*, 219–23).

reform. In his sermon at his installation, he declared, "I need you!" He needs us not as subordinates but, as his own Episcopal motto puts it, as "co-workers in the truth" of the gospel.

This joint work must prove itself in many areas. I am thinking of participation and subsidiarity in church life, of the issue of the *ethos* for a future European world politics, but also of the AIDS ministry in Africa and above all of the sacrifices on behalf of the poor called for in the Latin American church. This option for the poor compels the European church to speak not only of the redemption of the guilty, but also of God's justice for those who are innocent and suffer unjustly. The Church must follow Jesus in his fundamental sensitivity to the suffering of others. Confronting this issue will be the Petrine service of Benedict XVI.

SZ: In 1979, Cardinal Ratzinger, as Archbishop of Munich, blocked your appointment to the faculty at University of Munich. Don't you hold that against him?

JBM: At first, yes. When I met Ratzinger at the 1980 Berlin Catholic Day after his intervention against me, I had recovered my composure. He asked, "Are you going to shoot me now?" and I answered, "You know that priests don't carry pistols." Although he invited me to Munich for a conversation, we didn't meet for many years. Without my knowledge, some of my Münster colleagues invited Cardinal Ratzinger to a symposium celebrating my seventieth birthday in August of 1998. When I found out, I seriously doubted that he would accept the invitation, that he could come. But come he did. As he explained in a letter, he wanted "to resume the dialogue with Johann Baptist Metz." Is it any wonder, then, that I believe he's capable of surprises in his new post?

SZ: Until the meeting in Westphalia, at Ahaus, you two were considered polar opposites: here the servant of the institutional church and critic of liberation themes, there the critic of the institution and proponent of liberating base communities. You have borrowed from that neo-Marxism which Ratzinger rejected in principle. Was this polarity, seen in retrospect, not as harsh as it once seemed?

JBM: In the light of our contemporary world situation, there is first and foremost a basic theological commonality: the pluralism of religious and cultural worlds, dramatically intensified by globalization, does not allow us to dispense with the question of truth. Certainly Ratzinger and I spoke and still speak different languages: I doubt that the question of truth in theology, in speaking of God, can be rescued only through Platonism and Idealism. The theology of Benedict seems to suggest just this. Whereas I (on the contrary) have always attempted to sustain the truth by passing through the critical spirit of the Enlightenment and post-Idealistic philosophies—somewhat along the lines of a negative metaphysics that was at home with the early Frankfurt School, as I keep reminding my friend, Jürgen Habermas.

The fundamental structure of the new political theology is shaped by *memoria passionis*, by remembering suffering and those who suffer. Accordingly, its idea of reason isn't indifferent to morality. This reason doesn't want to create the world of morality but rather is—as a condition of its autonomy—*a priori* involved in the world of morality. In critical continuation of the primacy of a practical reason, its autonomy will be rooted in a type of acknowledgement: unconditionally recognizing the authority of those who are innocent and suffer unjustly. Only this authority of those who suffer prevents reason from being instrumentalized. So I call for "reason with an *a priori* of suffering." History as a Grand Narrative only exists as a history of human suffering.

I have never understood autonomy and emancipation as an abstract denial of obedience or an absolute negation of all authority, but rather as unconditional respect for one particular authority, namely, the authority of those who suffer. Whoever refuses to obey this authority confuses autonomy with narcissism and emancipation with caprice. The authority of those who suffer is in my view also the inner authority of a world morality which binds all human beings and which no religion, no church, may subvert or relativize.

SZ: The English historian Timothy Garton Ash has put forth the opinion "Atheists should applaud the election of Benedict XVI because this old, scholarly, conservative, and uncharismatic Bavarian theologian will accelerate de-Christianization in Europe even if he intends the opposite." Could Ash be right?

JBM: There could of course be new categories and distinctions within Catholicism—though hardly in the sense Ash suggests. Unfortunately, even he could not free himself from the negative Ratzinger clichés of the British tabloids. Moreover, a peculiar notion of charisma underlies his assessment. Did the charisma that he imputes to the late pope and denies to the new pope really prevent the creeping de-Christianization of Europe?

SZ: Why do the Germans judge Ratzinger so critically and even call him a fundamentalist?

JBM: With the "liberalization" of theology here—a theology which often seems to be more provincial than it would like to admit—a historically pent-up anti-Roman feeling has grown even stronger. Moving beyond this trench warfare with Rome was, by the way, the motive of my colleagues when they invited Ratzinger to Ahaus in 1998.

Benedict XVI is not a fundamentalist because fundamentalists don't reflect on their convictions. Those who call him a fundamentalist are probably those same people who are themselves, in his eyes, fundamentalists of the arbitrary, obedient to that "dictatorship of relativism" which he denounced in his speech to the conclave. It seems to me to be more appropriate to talk about the "sweet poison" of relativism. This poison wants increasingly to paralyze our readiness to hold something as so important, so holy for life, that we do not open it for discussion either in modern discourse or in the postmodern pluralism of opinions and voices.

SZ: From the beginning, Benedict XVI has emphasized that he wants to stress ecumenism. How could that happen concretely?

JBM: Ecumenism among Christians must be rooted in ecumenism between Christians and Jews. The ecumenical movement among Christians will only succeed when they retrieve their biblical-messianic perspective. Here the late pope has laid out important markers for "the Church after Auschwitz." Benedict XVI should follow his lead.

SZ: You have continually expressed your shock that "in our Christian speech about God the history of human suffering which cries out to heaven is so little heard and seen." Christianity must "achieve sympathetic awareness of the suffering of others." Do you believe you have in Benedict XVI an ally for attaining this "compassion"?

JBM: Compassion is the positive answer to the question: Is there a way of dealing with today's pluralism of religions that is open to and reasonable for all? In the universally acknowledged diversity of religions and cultures, there is one true criterion for understanding and cooperation that binds us all. In a time of latent religious and cultural struggles there is this offer of global peace from Christianity. A Christianity which understands its own roots always has to do with compassion. I would like to have the pope on my side in this program for our world, but meanwhile I am grateful I don't have to count him as opposed to it from the beginning.

SZ: Your most famous term is surely "God crisis." Today, one often speaks of a renaissance of faith. Is the God crisis history?

JBM: The God crisis is not identical with a crisis of religion; in fact it is often immersed in a religion-friendly atmosphere. A religious atmosphere is affirmed, but God's demands are denied. Also, this denial is not really meant categorically as in the sense of the great passionate atheisms. Atheism in the time of the God crisis has become banal.

One can and should, however, expect the young to accept the demands and not just the comfort of Christianity. To whom else should one entrust this adventurous idea of being there for others, without receiving anything in return? To whom can one offer the way of life this implies, if not to young people? Compassion is not for the old.

SZ: Will the Catholic Church of the future be a small flock, a community of a few "true believers" or a powerful, growing, worldwide community?

JBM: The Catholic Church will never be a small flock in the sense of a seemingly fundamentalist sect; her own message keeps her from that path. Maybe she will become a more scattered flock than before. The Church, the oldest global institution of humankind, is present around the world today, but more and more in a global diaspora. I have previously attempted to put forth the picture of the Church as a Catholic elephant.

I would like to direct questions connected with such an image to our new pope: What would happen if this elephant, if this church of millions and millions of people, would dare this experiment of compassion, of the empathy which springs from our passion for God, even in a small and insignificant way? What if the church did it all-out, undaunted, so that this experiment could infuse the foundations of our life together? What would happen if an ecumenism of compassion arose among all Christians—would not faith throw a new light on this world so full of sorrow and torn by the storms of globalization?

Translated by John K. Downey

CHAPTER 10

Wake Up, Open Your Eyes, See the Suffering

Aachener Zeitung[1]: What is political theology?

JBM: It's theology—and nothing else. It is the attempt to speak of God in these times, that is, to talk about God while facing the world, with all its social and historical challenges.

AZ: So the focus lies more on "theology" than on "political."

JBM: Yes.

AZ: But facing the world. So is a political theologian then also a liberation theologian?

JBM: The idea of political theology is very old. It comes from ancient traditions. This was a very conservative category. The new political theology, on the other hand, tries to incorporate the principles of the political Enlightenment into theology, to deal with these and with the modern pluralistic world.

AZ: The Peruvian Father Gustavo Gutiérrez, founder of liberation theology, pointed out the timeliness of liberation theology a few

1. Interview conducted by Peter Rappert (Metz, *Gespräche, Interviews, Antworten,* 210–14).

weeks ago. What does the importance of the struggle against poverty and discrimination mean for the church?

JBM: The Latin American church dedicated itself to this option for the poor over thirty years ago. Gutiérrez is a good friend; he has incorporated political theology's critical questioning of ideology into his dialogical liberation approach: Who does theology, in whose interest, in what circumstances, and for what audience? Also, Gutiérrez understands the church as an institution of the socially critical freedom of faith and wants to make it clear that the message of Jesus is about all of our world. At its core, the biblical mysticism of Christianity is a political mysticism, which I call a mysticism of open eyes. It is not God, not Christ, not truth, not peace that are the most frequent words of the Bible, but wake up, open your eyes. The option for the poor plays a very large role in today's storms of globalization.

AZ: Has the fierce inner-church controversy over liberation theology subsided?

JBM: The controversy has subsided since the critics of liberation theologians have realized the following: For most liberation theologians, the tie to a Marxist-socialist concept was so close that the political fate of this concept resulted in the loss of its significance for their theology as well.

AZ: Does a different development also play a part? Some Vatican cognoscenti argue that the pope is as critical of globalized, unleashed capitalism as he is of the old communism.

JBM: One could say that.

AZ: Then the pope himself may be a liberation theologian.

JBM: Well, when you stretch words too much they lose their meaning and history. In the words "liberation theology," especially when dealing with people at the grassroots level, with the liberation of communities, there is so much adversity, so much pain and suffering that one should not use that label abstractly. It has its own history and dignity. One should not globalize this phrase. It applies where it is really existentially about liberation. Liberation is no Punch and Judy show.

AZ: Millions of people around the world are still being persecuted, abused, oppressed. The strong, the rich, and the powerful can't manage to help them. What does the promise that the last shall be the first bring to the afflicted?

JBM: The bourgeois world must have its eyes forced open. There is a duty to see the suffering of others. It is precisely those people who call themselves Christians who must show solidarity.

AZ: But back to my question—formulated differently: In God's creation many innocent people suffer. Is this God's justice? Is this compassion?

JBM: That is the basic question. That's why the *topos* of Auschwitz played such a large role in my theology. On the questions of whether it is still possible to pray after Auschwitz, I have always replied that we can still pray after Auschwitz because in Auschwitz itself there was prayer. We owe the future of prayer to the people who prayed even in that hell. The language of human beings in the face of such unspeakable suffering is not theology. More likely their language is the dream or the story and, above all, the cry and the prayer. My own considered opinion is: Christianity, if it takes itself seriously, does not, in its so-called theodicy question—that is, the question of God's justice, of the innocent suffering in God's creation—have an answer, but rather one more question. This question of justice troubles us too little. It has no answer, but only a hope.

AZ: Hope doesn't help many people, not the children who are sent into the mines or forced into prostitution today. And the question

arises over and over again among believing and non-believing peo-
ple: Can't God override such crimes, or does God not want to?

JBM: That's a Greek question, if I may say so—

AZ: The question of Epicurus.

JBM: Exactly. There is a great Greek philosophical tradition of this
question: God and the evil in the world. This question has come to
be seen as unanswerable at least since Kant. Philosophy does not
tolerate unanswerable questions. Christianity on the other hand is a
religion of unanswered questions. How can one begin to pray, if academic speech "about God" does not become a question "for God,"
a crying out "to God"? I certainly can't justify God myself: I am not
above God. Biblical and Christian hope means banking on God's
future, giving God the chance to justify himself "in his day." This
hope knows pain and grief to the limits of despair. It is anything but
a childish optimism. Paul spoke of it as "hoping against all hope": it
is governed by the principles of practical reason.

AZ: Should one be surprised that more people have not become athe-
ists as a result of Auschwitz?

JBM: That may be. The question is whether there is an authority
whom one can question or rather to whom one can cry out, or if
the only response to the misery in the world is oblivion, if happiness is bought by cultural amnesia, that is, whether happiness
is built on the forgotten victims of history. Human beings carry
within them a profound cry for justice. They feel that they can no
longer be happy in the face of the great misery of others.

AZ: This brings us to a crucial point of your theology, namely, sensi-
tivity to the suffering of others. You call it "compassion" (Mitleiden-
shaft). And you link the question of suffering in God's creation—the
theodicy question—to the dialogue among religions.

JBM: The empathetic awareness of others' suffering is the basic category of Christian talk about God. I deliberately don't want to call it pity (*Mitleid*).[2] You cannot deny that both Christianity and Judaism want to say something to all people. And this goes for the dialogue among the world's religions, as well. In this dialogue too, with all tolerance, we can and must insist on the truth. It is more difficult to defend established truth than to find truth. But such is religion. That's what you have to answer for. No religion claiming to be part of the high culture of our time can evade the obligation to see other people's suffering. This cannot be relativized. That is why I speak of the authority of those who suffer, which prior to any vote, prior to any rapprochement, obliges all people, and which therefore cannot be betrayed or relativized by any religion or culture worthy of these names—not even the church. In my opinion, this authority of the suffering must be the criterion for all religious and cultural dialogues.

AZ: And that's why you are critical of Hans Küng's "Global Ethics" project?

JBM: Yes, because you can't define a global ethic by vote. A global ethic must have its own authority. A minimal consensus is not enough.

AZ: So, in your opinion, Küng is doing it the wrong way around?

JBM: He's not doing theology but religious politics. That's commendable. I am not against talking about global ethics. But how do we define it? The authority of a global ethic must be the authority of those who are innocent and suffer unjustly. If that is the case, we should check whether in the eyes of people today there is a religion that deserves the name.

2. Although it is not so visible in translation, Metz often uses the English word "compassion" in his German texts in order to highlight his very particular notion and to avoid the overtones of German words such as *Mitleid*. [Ed.]

AZ: Your idea is very ambitious, very demanding. It comes at a time of a certain lack of religious commitment. Are you worried about that?

JBM: You could say that. The church crisis is relatively harmless. The real problem is the crisis of God. We no longer live in the time when they said, "Jesus, yes—church, no," but rather in a time in which they say, "Religion, yes—God, no." That's what I call religion-friendly godlessness. Norbert Blüm said in 1989, "Marx is dead, Jesus lives." I told him, "Wouldn't it be nice. Unfortunately, the sentence must read: "Marx is dead, Nietzsche lives." We live in postmodern times: many new religions are blooming on the grave of God, as Nietzsche predicted. In this pluralism, religion is at most a matter of "which one."

AZ: Does this also refer to the popularity of Buddhism in this country?

JBM: In meeting with members of Asian religions, I encountered a great deal of skepticism on the part of original Buddhists toward "Western Buddhism." You can't just mimic what they do. They don't want that, either. The Buddhism fashionable in our country is turning into "religion light." And that's not even Buddhism. In dealing with the question of suffering, of course Buddhists withdraw into meditation and silence. They seek the dissolution of the ego in the harmony of the universe. A Buddhist mysticism of suffering is a mysticism of nature, a mysticism without a subject, without a face. But this is not the attitude of Jesus. His earthly history ended with an apocalyptic cry.

Translated by John K. Downey

CHAPTER 11

Remembering Johann Baptist Metz

J. Matthew Ashley[1]

In the last desperate weeks of World War II in Germany, a sixteen-year-old soldier was sent by his commanding officer to the rear with a message for headquarters. When he returned, he found the other members of his unit, all as young as he, dead, wiped out in a sudden air and armored assault.

"Now," he remembered, "I could only see dead and empty faces, where the day before I had shared childhood fears and laughter. I remember nothing but a wordless cry. This is how I see myself to this very day, and behind this memory all of my childhood dreams crumble away. . . . What would happen if one took this sort of thing not to the psychologist but into the church, and if one would not allow oneself to be talked out of such unreconciled memories even by theology, but rather wanted to have faith with them, and with them to speak about God?"

This young man was Johann Baptist Metz, and he went on to do just this, becoming in the process a trail-blazing theologian for an age in which memories like these have become far too common and, what is worse, met with ever greater indifference. He died on December 2 [2019] at the age of ninety-one.

---

1. First published in *America Magazine*, December 3, 2019.

Metz (Baptist to his friends) was born in Auerbach, in north-east Bavaria, on August 5, 1928. It was a small Catholic town, not yet touched by the processes of secularization at work in the rest of Europe. As he once wrote, "One comes from far away when one comes from there. It is as if one were born not fifty years ago, but somewhere along the receding edges of the Middle Ages."

While the town was very Catholic, he did not remember his family being particularly pious—he once joked that of all the seminarians studying with him when he started in Bamberg, he was the only one who had not been an altar boy. His schooling was interrupted when he was forced into the Wehrmacht. And after the attack on his unit, he was captured and spent seven months in POW camps on the East Coast of the United States (and so he spoke English with a distinctly American accent).

Sent back to Germany, he finished his final two years of Gymnasium (high school) in one year and entered the diocesan seminary in Bamberg. His bishop had intended to send him to Rome for further training, but Metz persuaded him to send him to the recently refounded Jesuit seminary in Innsbruck instead, because he had been impressed by reading some writings by one of its faculty—Karl Rahner, SJ, one of the most important Catholic theologians of the twentieth century, who became a key theological advisor at Vatican II. In Innsbruck, he earned a doctorate in philosophy and then in theology. He was ordained a priest in 1954.

During his years at Innsbruck, he became Rahner's student, friend, and later, collaborator. Rahner left a deep and enduring impact on the young theologian-in-training, an impact that went far beyond the academic: Metz called him simply, "my father in faith." Even though his theology took a different direction than his teacher's after 1963, Metz always referred to him as his principal theological inspiration.

In 1963 Metz took up a position at the University of Münster. In 1979 he was offered a prestigious position at the University of Munich, where Romano Guardini and then Rahner had taught earlier. But his appointment was vetoed by the then-Archbishop of

Munich, Joseph Ratzinger (which led Rahner to write a fiery open letter in a German periodical: "I Protest").

So Metz remained at the University of Münster, where he taught for thirty years. After retiring in 1993, he was a visiting professor at the University of Vienna for four years, before returning to Münster, where he lived and continued to work until his death.

Like so many of his generation, he took as his theological labor interpreting and promoting the theological riches of Vatican II. Along with Rahner, Edward Schillebeeckx, OP, and others, he was a cofounder of the journal *Concilium*, which had this purpose.

For him, in particular, this work meant helping the Catholic Church make the transition from the seamlessly Catholic world of Auerbach to the techno-scientific, multicultural, religiously pluralistic and often secularized world of today. In the 1960s he became one of the founders, along with Jürgen Moltmann and Dorothee Sölle, of a theological approach called "political theology," which he himself named the new political theology in order to distinguish it from the work of Nazi legal theorist, Carl Schmitt.

Political theology was a prophetic protest against the privatization of Christian faith: the reduction of its scope to one's relationship to God and one-on-one ethical behavior toward others. For Metz, religion in general, and Christianity in particular, is inherently political.

So too is Christian theology. Christianity's privatization, Metz warned, is a principal way that it has been domesticated in the modern world, with the church too often going along, explicitly or tacitly. Yet Christian faith was not for him simply a source of meaning or a social glue in society; it was not a kind of sacred canopy, as sociologist Peter Berger once put it, a religious authorization or echo of what is going on in society anyway.

Religion is, rather, for Metz, provocative and interruptive. It breaks through our self-reliance and self-satisfaction, attitudes often purchased at the cost of ignoring the suffering of those put on the margins of society or who had been left beaten on the side of the road in its march of progress.

Remembering them is dangerous, but these dangerous memories are liberating. And they are ultimately sustained by the dangerous memory of Jesus Christ, who died and was raised by the God of the living and of the dead. It is a memory that can give rise to great hope, but only if it is put into practice, a "combative hope," as Pope Francis puts it.

Metz followed these insights with thoroughness and integrity, realizing that for a German the dangerous memory above all others had to be the memory of the Jews and the fate they suffered under the Third Reich. He will be remembered for insisting that Christian identity "after Auschwitz" can only be reconstructed and saved together with the Jews and by retrieving the lost or suppressed roots of Christian faith in Judaism.

He will also be remembered for insisting on the importance of spirituality, not only for Christian faith, but for theology itself. One of his early writings, *Poverty of Spirit*, a spiritual classic, is still in print over fifty years after its publication in 1963. He wrote compellingly about the contribution of religious orders in the church, and recently he wrote of the importance of a "mysticism of open eyes," open to the suffering of others. He mourned the ways that the church has itself created victims but confessed as well that he knew of no way that a genuinely Christian hope could be sustained in today's culture without an institutional bearer that would stand up for it and represent it. His was not an "easy" or "comforting" theology; but one that provoked, inspired, gave hope.

It is fitting that Metz died on December 2, the thirty-ninth anniversary of the murder of four US women missionaries by a terrorist government in El Salvador. For Metz, both faith and theology only achieve their full stature in solidarity with victims and as witnesses to hope against hope. Likewise, it is fitting that he died at the beginning of Advent, the season of hope. He took his definition of theology not from Anselm's "faith seeking understanding," but from the first letter of Peter: "Always be ready to make your defense to anyone who demands from you an accounting of the hope that is in you" (2 Pet 3:15).

If Dietrich Bonhoeffer warned against the dangers of cheap grace, perhaps Metz will be remembered for his prophetic warnings against cheap hope: the thin hopes of a consumer culture that, Metz complained, has even abandoned its secular heritage from the Enlightenment of hoping for freedom, equality, and fraternity for all humankind.

But he also warned against the narrow Christian hope of one's individual survival after death. Neither will ultimately console.

The great hopes and the great biblical images of hope, Metz insisted, can only be hoped for others. Only when we hope them for others and act out of that hope, he maintained, can we hope them for ourselves.

Bibliography

Ashley, Matthew M. *Interruptions: Mysticism, Politics, and Theology in the Work of Johann Baptist Metz*. Notre Dame: University of Notre Dame Press, 1998.

———. "Remembering Johann Baptist Metz." *America: The Jesuit Review*, December 3, 2019. https://www.americamagazine.org/arts-culture/2019/12/03/remembering-johann-baptist-metz.

Bernhardt, Uwe. "Die Kehrseite des abendländischen Geistes." *Merkur* 43 (1931).

Blumenberg, Hans. *Säkularisierung und Selbsbehauptung*. Frankfurt: Suhrkamp, 1974.

Casanova, José. "Der Ort der Religion in säkularen Europa." *Transit* 27 (2004).

Christakis, Nicholas A. *Blueprint: The Evolutionary Origins of a Good Society*. New York: Little, Brown Spark, 2019.

Enzensberger, Hans Magnus. "Gedankenflucht (1)." In *Kiosk: Neue Gedichte*. Frankfurt: Suhrkamp, 1995.

Goldhagen, Daniel. *Hitler's Willing Executioners: Ordinary Germans and the Holocaust*. New York: Alfred A. Knopf, 1996.

Gross, Walter, and Karl-Josef Kuschel. *"Ich schaffe Finsternis und Heil": Ist Gott verantwortlich für des Übel?* Mainz: Matthias Grünewald, 1992.

Habermas, Jürgen. "Israel und Athen oder: Wem gehört die anamnetische Vernunft?" In *Diagnosen zur Zeit*, edited by Johann Baptist Metz et al., 57–64. Düsseldorf: Patmos, 1994.

———. *The Liberating Power of Symbols: Philosophical Essays*. Cambridge: Polity, 2001.

———. *Zwischen Naturalismus und Religion*. Frankfurt: Suhrkamp, 2005.

Manemann, Jürgen. *Carl Schmitt und die Politische Theologie*. Münster: Lit Verlag, 2002.

Martinez, Gaspar. *Confronting the Mystery of God: Political, Liberation, and Public Theologies*. New York: Continuum, 2001.

Metz, Johann Baptist. "Compassion: Zu einem Weltprogramm des Chrsiten-
tums im Zeitalter des Pluralismus der Religionem und Kulturen." In
Compassion: Weltprogramm des Christentums, edited by Lothar Kuld,
Johann Baptist Metz, and Adolf Weisbrod, 9–18. Freiburg: Herder, 2000.
———. "The Elephant with Hope." Interview by Michael Jackqueman.
Translated by John K. Downey. *Katholische Nachrichten-Agentur*
(November 23, 2000) 1–2.
———. "Facing the Jews." In *Faith and the Future: Essays on Theology, Solidarity,
and Modernity*, edited by Johann Baptist Metz and Jürgen Moltmann, 38–
48. Maryknoll: Orbis, 1995.
———. *Faith in History and Society: Toward a Practical Fundamental Theology*.
Translated by J. Matthew Ashley. New York: Crossroad, 2007.
———. *Gespräche, Interviews, Antworten: Eine Auswahl*. Vol. 8 of *Gesammelte
Schriften*, edited by Johann Reikerstorfer. Freiburg: Herder, 2017.
———. *Glaube in Geschichte und Gesellschaft: Studien zu einer prakischen
fundamental Theologie*. Mainz: Mattias Grünewald, 1992.
———. "Karl Rahner—ein theologisches Leben: Theologie als mystische
Biographie eines Christenmenschen." *Stimmen der Zeit* 192 (1974) 305–
14.
———, ed. *"Landschaft aus Schreien": Zur Dramatik der Theodizeefrage*. Mainz:
Matthias Grünewald, 1995.
———. *Memoria Passionis: Ein provozierendes Gedächtnis in pluralistischer
Gesellschaft*. Freiburg: Herder, 2006.
———. "On God and Happiness." Interview by Jürgen Manemann. Translated
by John K. Downey. *Theologie der Gegenwart* 49.2 (2006) 124–25.
———. "Politische Theologie." In Vol. 8, *Lexikon für Theologie und Kirche*,
edited by Walter Kasper, 392–94. 3rd ed. Freiburg: Herder, 1999.
———. "'Politische Theologie' in der Diskussion." In *Diskussion zur politischen
Theologie*, edited by Helmut Peukert, 267–301. Mainz: Mattias Grünewald,
1969.
———. "Suffering unto God." Translated by J. Matthew Ashley. *Critical Inquiry*
20.4 (1994) 611–22.
———. *Theology of the World*. New York: Seabury, 1973.
———. *Unterbrechungen: Theologisch-politische Perspektiven und Profile*.
Gütersloh: Gütersloh Verlagshaus, 1982.
———. "Vernunft mit Leidensapriori." In *Vernunftfähiger—vernunftbedürftiger
Glaube*, edited by Kurt Appel, Wolfgang Treitler, and Peter Zellinger, 25–
31. Frankfurt: Peter Lang, 2005.
———. "Zukunft aus dem Gedächtnis des Leidens. Eine gegenwärtige Gestalt der
Verantwortung des Glaubens." *Concilium* 8 (1972) 399–407.
———. *Zum Begriff der neuen Politischen Theologie: 1967–1997*. Mainz:
Matthias Grünewalt, 1997.
Nietzsche, Friedrich. *Basic Writings*. Edited and translated by Walter Kaufmann.
New York: Modern Library, 1968.

————. *The Use and Abuse of History*. Translated by Adrian Collins. 2nd ed. Indianapolis: Bobbs-Merrill, 1980.

Peters, Tiemo R. *Johann Baptist Metz: Theologie des vermißten Gottes*. Mainz: Mattias Grünewald, 1998.

————. "Karl Rahner und die neue Politische Theologie." In *Hundert Jahre Karl Rahner*, edited by Heinrich Klauke, 43–50. Cologne: Karl Rahner Akademie, 2004.

Rahner, Karl. "Why Does God Let Us Suffer?" In Vol. 19, *Theological Investigations*, 194–208. Translated by Edward Quinn. New York: Crossroad, 1983.

Reikerstorfer, Johann. "Im 'Theodizeeblick': Die neue Politische Theologie von Johann Baptist Metz." In *Theologien der Gegenwart: eine Einführung*. Darmstadt: Wissenschaftliche Buchgesellschaft, 2006.

————. "Jüdisch-christliches Erbe in vernunfttheoretischer Bedeutung bei J. Habermas und J.B. Metz." *Orientierung* 70.3 (2006) 30–34.

Sapolsky, Robert M. *Behave: The Biology of Humans at Our Best and Worst*. New York: Penguin, 2017.

Weiler, Joseph H. H. *Ein christliches Europa*. Salzburg: Anton Pustet, 2004.

Weinrich, Harald. *Lethe: Kunst und Kritik des Vergessens*. Munich: C. H. Beck, 1997.

Zamora, José A. *Krise, Kritik, Erinnerung*. Münster: Lit Verlag, 1995.